Rocking the Ages

THE PULSE OF CONTINUITY AND CHANGE

Rocking the Ages

THE PULSE OF CONTINUITY AND CHANGE

Edited by Carol S. Lawson & Robert F. Lawson

CHRYSALIS BOOKS / *Swedenborg Foundation Publishers*
West Chester, Pennsylvania

THE CHRYSALIS READER is a book series that examines themes related to the universal quest for wisdom. Inspired by the Swedenborg Foundation journal *Chrysalis,* each volume presents original short stories, essays, poetry, and art exploring the spiritual dimensions of a chosen theme. Works are selected by the series editors. For information on future themes or submission of original writings, contact Carol S. Lawson, Route 1, Box 184, Dillwyn, Virginia 23936.

© 2000 by the Swedenborg Foundation

All rights reserved.

No part of this book may be reproduced or transmitted in any form or by any means, electronic or mechanical, including photocopying, recording, or any information storage or retrieval system, without prior permission from the publisher, except in the case of brief quotations embodied in critical articles and reviews.

Printed on recycled paper and bound in the United States of America.

LIBRARY OF CONGRESS CATALOGING-IN-PUBLICATION DATA
Rocking the Ages: the pulse of continuity and change / edited by Carol S. Lawson & Robert F. Lawson
   p.   cm. — (Chrysalis Reader; v. 7)
ISBN 0-87785-231-6
1. Aging—Literary collections.   2. Maturation (Psychology)—Literary collections.   3. Life change events—Literary collections.   4. Life cycle, Human—Literary collections.   5. American literature—20th century.
I. Lawson, Carol S.   II. Lawson, Robert F., 1948–   .   III. Series
PS509.A37 R63 2000
810.8'0354—dc21
00-064360

 CHRYSALIS BOOKS
Swedenborg Foundation Publishers
320 North Church Street
West Chester, Pennsylvania 19380

Contents

EDITOR'S NOTES
Dark Matter (poem) viii
    Tom O'Grady
This Millennial Passage ix
    Robert F. Lawson

FOREWORD
Wrestling with the Speech of Angels xii
    Stuart Shotwell

PART I: BETWEEN WORLDS
Rhythms of Repercussion 5
    Anders Hallengren
For Alan at Fifty-three (poem) 23
    Arlene Distler
When the Princess Died (fiction) 24
    Pamela Mayer
Sick Infant, Recovered (poem) 34
    Ethan Gilsdorf
My Finite Eyes 36
    Wesley McNair
For an Ancient Artist (poem) 40
    Steven Lautermilch
The Call of Stone 42
    John Hitchcock
Archaeologists (cartoon) 47
    Mike Taylor
Pittsburgh—Revisited 48
    Rosalind Baker Wilson

PART II: GENERATIONAL CONSTELLATIONS
The Woman Who Uttered Paradise (poem) 54
    Elizabeth Oakes
That's All Right, Mama 55
    Marsha Dubrow
Facets of Truth 59
    Eve Baker
The Naming 65
    Jan Frazier
The Wedding (fiction) 69
    Angie Pelekidis
If Winter Comes 80
    Donald L. Rose

What Could Be Better? 81
  Rebecca A. Hall
Surry County (poem) 86
  Keppel Hagerman

PART III: ROUNDABOUT

Star of the East (poem) 89
  William Kloefkorn
To the Center and Back 91
  Forster Freeman
A Magical Tradition: Neo-Paganism 95
  Karen Everson
Uneasy Alliance (poem) 101
  Pat Schneider
The Age of Addiction 103
  Rae Hallstrom
The Point of Spring 108
  M. Garrett Bauman
This November Day (poem) 111
  Elisa Leigh

PART IV: COMING OF AGE

The Harvesters 115
  Michael Nethercott
Forged and Tempered (fiction) 118
  James Ward
Pageant (poem) 125
  Virgil Suarez
Spiritual Eldering 126
  Roberta Bolduc
First Flight 130
  Edward DeRegibus
Melon Soup (poem) 133
  Carol Lem

PART V: EXUBERANT SEASONS

June, 1941 (poem) 136
  Beverly Fleming
Communication Tongued with Fire: My Encounter with T. S. Eliot .. 138
  John Wren–Lewis
Home on the Range (fiction) 146
  Loraine Campbell
The Hills Near Darky, Wisconsin (poem) 151
  Robert Bly
Growing Up in Wisconsin 152
  Joseph H. Foegen and Susan Foegen
Pittsburgh in 1950 (poem) 158
  Thomas Kretz

Silent Messenger 160
   Lani Wright
The Seaman (poem) 162
   James Rensenbrink

PART VI: THROUGH A MIRROR DARKLY

Going Beyond Copernicus 165
   Sarah Voss
Good for Business (fiction) 172
   Rita Quinton
Angle of Light in Late Fall (poem) 179
   Alan Yount
Introducing a New Science of Soul 181
   Robert Keck

TOM O'GRADY

Dark Matter
for Ryan

In the birthday myth the tree is not cut
but split along its lonely body
so that you may enter it unclothed, at night,
yet dressed, as the night is dressed, in a secret fire
of descending, coloring, shadows of light
lit by the dim moon or the lace of stars.
And entering you will flower,
like figures on a vase,
as we are all flowers
fermenting into bloom.
And the violins within will sing, although
it is a dark matter, this unseen universe before us
and the longitudes of true place
that may, or may not, exist.
And leaving on the other side
you may cross pastures and enter a stream
to wash the sap from your limbs
and lie out in the new grasses
until, clothed in solitude,
you rise up to begin still another year
elsewhere and not where you began.
That is gone now.
The land stretches quietly before you;
the sea keeps to itself;
but the sky opens,
the sky opens wide above.

TOM O'GRADY is editor of the *Hampden-Sydney Poetry Review* and Poet-in-Residence at Hampden-Sydney College in Virginia.

EDITOR'S NOTES: ROBERT F. LAWSON

This Millennial Passage

I'M SITTING IN A CHINESE RESTAURANT overlooking the Connecticut River and its wide valley of ancient trees. Alone and hungry, I am tantalized by the aroma of exotic dishes around me and find myself jolted from my reverie by a stimulating birthday celebration at a neighboring table. Looking out the window, I realize in this millennial year that we are also between seasons. A soft, steady spring rain settles the evening. A mist covers the verdant meadow. We are months, years it seems, from the dry rustle of fall leaves and the crackle of September grasses. I also know this Chrysalis will require a season of growth and harvest before these and the thoughts of others will be bound in a book. And so it is with life. We are constantly reminded of the fluid nature, the hydrologic cycle, of living in a temporal environment—a stone, half submerged in a brook. *Rocking the Ages* holds essays and stories, poetry and art that revolve around our perceptions of time and place. As a collective voice, they ask, "In a world of which it is said the only constant is change, what is permanent?"

IN PART I, "BETWEEN WORLDS," we travel with the in-between people who are shedding their skins. We find a man at midlife who struggles with the ethos of a whale out of its element; we stand with a photographer before ancient rock art in Utah and with a philosopher before an ancient stone circle in Britain; we behold the miracle of an infant who lightly touches down on this earthly plane, leaves for a time and then returns. And in this place of slow moving water and iridescent starlight, we resonate with the chords of an inner world of music, are led by children to see more clearly our own simple truths.

FAMILY RELATIONSHIPS tied to singular events occur in Part II, "Generational Constellations." We glimpse in this section planetary transits—the advent of rock and roll in the living room, an annual trek to a Civil War graveyard, attending a Greek wedding, carrying a loved one's memory in a name, holding an heirloom and wondering where the truth lies in family legend. Here we dwell on the dynamic of fathers and daughters, of mothers and sons, a father who goes fishing with his son-in-law, and over this arbor of humanity, we breathe the magic of morning and evening blooms.

WHETHER IT'S through a neo-pagan dance, a farming chore gone awry, or a Christmas Eve celebration—recycling at different levels occurs in Part III, "Roundabout." We all must come to terms at some point with the ritual walks, the labyrinths in our lives that lead to the center and back. Feeling the change from winter's pent-up madness to the spirited flow of springtime, watching the interaction of animal life as it crosses our path, knowing we must guard against grasping for what is unattainable, we can let the sand tick through cupped hands, come to appreciate the time-honored lesson that what goes around, comes around.

WHAT COMES OF OUR FIRST FLIGHTS—and our returnings? Of standing up to an act of inhumanity, responding to aging generations warehoused in rest homes, accepting the reality of family tradition in all of its totality? In Part IV, "Coming of Age," pivotal events of personal growth are explored. These are the stored events that build the narrative of our lives. This is the stuff of retaliation and redemption, the working reality of a blue-collar bar, the finishing mill of a girl's beauty pageant, all retold at tribal gatherings after the hunt.

CELEBRATIONS OF LIFE are witnessed in Part V, "Exuberant Seasons," times when we are living fully in the moment, when time and space fall away. We examine a snapshot of a family unit—still intact in the viewer's mind, are amused by a father's enchantment with the American past despite suburbia's encroachments, relive an academic's encounter with a classic poet, pull to the side of the road for a luna moth caught in the crossfire of traffic. And whether it happened a hundred years ago in a small Wisconsin town, fifty years ago in Pittsburgh, or today on a spring outing to forested hills waking from winter, these energizing pellets of time propel us forward on our journey.

THE FINAL COLLECTION OF WRITING IN PART VI, "Through a Mirror Darkly," banks, like venture capital, on the unknown. Here we move off the map in radical trajectories that take us beyond Copernicus to new models of consciousness, to extrapolations based on an attempt to control aberrant behavior through the use of chemicals, to watery realms where memory is suspended like last year's season of leaves and mud. We come up for air, breaking the surface of hard-core science, in search of humanity's spiritual fire, in our quest for personal meaning and wholeness. We take in through these readings—these final, hypothetical slices of time—an altered light that shakes out some expectations and conjectures of what's good for us and others, that graphs the DNA tracings of the spirit, rehabilitating and enlarging our universe.

THERE IS ANOTHER PART OF THIS READER, an unnumbered Part VII. It is a current that flows through each part, which continues to ask, "What is permanent in all this change, this rocking of ages, this millenial passage?" If one were to ask the mystic Swedenborg, I think he would say the nature of change appears differently in the spiritual world—a place where, he reported, time and space are not set in motion by natural phenomena but directly correspond to one's spiritual receptivity. We can glimpse this omnipresent reality wherever we are. It's in this restaurant, in the faces of the diners, in the handshake of the owner who I am meeting for the first time. It's what ultimately drives the writing and art of this Chrysalis Reader—a loving presence of heart and mind, the pulse of continuity and change—that renews our place in the coming and going forth of humanity.

FOREWORD: STUART SHOTWELL

Wrestling with the Speech of Angels

Taller than the others, this man
Walked among them, at a distance,
Now and then calling the angels
By their secret names....
He knew, like the Greek, that the days
Of time are Eternity's mirrors.
In dry Latin he went on listing
The unconditional Last Things.
—JORGE LUIS BORGES,
translated by Richard Howard and Cesar Rennert

THE TASK IN WHICH I FIND MYSELF in this middle of my ages is full of contradictions and perplexities; but as I grapple with those difficulties, my life flexes and expands, like the muscles of a wrestler, now locked, now stretched, sometimes torn, but over time stronger and stronger.

This is the gist of the job: take twenty-five volumes of Latin written over two hundred years ago—which has until now been assumed to be "dry" even by lovers of literature as sensitive as the poet Borges—and wrestle it into an English that retains the emotional wealth and haunting simplicity of the original. To be precise, only a little of this task is mine; I work with a team of several translators, all of them more experienced than I am. The works in question are those of the eighteenth-century Swedish "researcher," Emanuel

Swedenborg (1688–1772), whom Borges describes so vividly in the epigraph above.

I call Swedenborg a researcher; the usual epithets are "scientist and seer," reflecting the two main ages of Swedenborg's life: the period in which he searched for the physical secrets of nature and the rewards of the world, including fame, and the period in which he looked beyond nature and transcended his craving for recognition. In the second of these ages, however, he remained as much a researcher as ever; he shifted his focus only in response to what he believed to be a divine leading.

My friends and family find my task incomprehensible and in a sense impossible. I see the question in their eyes when I tell them about it. How, they wonder, could anything written in that age—which to us, ever looking forward, seems ancient already—become fresh again for readers today? For them, the eighteenth century is dry and sere, an age that is gone forever.

Yet Swedenborg's era, the Enlightenment, was in fact a bodacious springtime in which the brash promises of the Renaissance at last had their fulfillment. Humankind had become aware once again of one of its most powerful tools, reason, and eagerly applied it to every subject beneath moon and sun, analyzing old hypotheses and coming to staggering new conclusions. Some used reason to test the Bible and declared it a hollow shell; others applied reason to hoary assumptions about government and law and decided monarchy was a baseless and unholy sham; others peered through reason's lens into science and saw new worlds swim into view in microscope and telescope. And yet it was also a time of tremendous spiritual renewal that went beyond the confines of reason into matters visionary and poetic.

Swedenborg was the arch-incarnation of the contradictory passions of this age, uniting its two distinct characteristics, rationality and spirituality. Confident that the time had come for these two to work together, he declared, "Now we are allowed to share in the mysteries of faith through the use of our intellect" (*True Christianity*, paragraph 508). The objects we see around us in everyday life—stones and stars, flowers and grasses, clothing and buildings—correspond to, one could even say in some manner vibrate in tune to, elements of the world beyond ours. Applying those "correspondences" as keys, the intellect can discern the truths hidden beyond the veil of the senses.

The skeptics of his day, bound by their reason, cast doubt on Swedenborg's visions. Yet even many who questioned his methods recognized that his works were a vast treasury of spiritual and poetic truths. Subsequent thinkers wandered awestruck into that treasury, drew heavily upon it, and never exhausted it; the roll call of their names reads like the list of honored guests at the feast of Western culture: Goethe, Blake, Balzac, Emerson, Strindberg, and Yeats are only a random half-dozen from the head table.

Yet hardly anyone knows of him today. The broad stream of Swedenborg's influence, though it has flowed through more than two centuries, is running underground and out of sight at the beginning of the twenty-first.

To those who have read Swedenborg lately, the reason behind this disappearance is pretty clear. The translations are too old; many are made up of revisions upon revisions of texts written originally by men who were alive in Swedenborg's day. Even some modern translations have preserved archaisms and dry, encrusted lumps of "Swedenborgianese" that are meaningless to readers now. All the translations, old and new, are filled with language that, in an unwitting offense to half the human race, consistently misrepresents Swedenborg's gender-inclusive style.

In short, our perception that the early translations of Swedenborg's works are dry and difficult is a result of the tension between disparate ages. The translators who brought Swedenborg's thought out of Latin into English in the eighteenth and nineteenth centuries were creatures of their age as we are of ours; and their translations no more suit us than would their clothing. If we want to have access to this treasury again, we have to find a way to make the springtime of Swedenborg's era blossom again in our own age.

How do we go about this? Bear with me for some theoretical considerations. Take this curious statement made by Swedenborg in the mid-1700s:

> There are two things that seem to be indispensable to our world, because they are inherent in nature: space and time. But in the world beyond ours, these two things do not matter, because there is no space or time, but *state* instead. There the *state of coming into existence* corresponds to what we call *time*. (condensed from *Arcana Coelestia,* paragraph 2625)

If this seems far-fetched, consider that one of the consequences of Einstein's theories is that for any particle moving at the speed of light, time does not exist. We may think that a photon that reaches us from a galaxy ten billion light-years away has traveled at the speed of light for ten billion years; but for the photon, no time has elapsed between its emission in some unknown star and the moment it strikes a sensor in the Hubble telescope. One physicist has even suggested that the entire universe is the weaving of a single particle, which transmutes itself instantaneously and infinitely into the dross and gold of countless suns and systems. The physicist's answer to the child who asks, "What was there before the universe existed?" is simply this: Nothing—because there never was a time before the universe existed: current physical theory strongly suggests that time itself did not exist before the material universe blossomed into being.

Like the physicist, Swedenborg says that beyond the world we see, there is no time, there is only a state that has something to do with *coming into existence,* with springing into being. Swedenborg was, in fact, very fond of a philosophical maxim current in his century to the effect that existing is not a static condition but a constant coming-into-being. Time, which we know as an inseparable part of life on earth, is only our dim mirror of an eternal state, which is a springing into existence. Or, to quote Borges again, who put it somewhat differently: "the days/Of time are Eternity's mirrors."

Our human perception of age, then, is faulty. An age, whether in the life of a civilization or an individual, is not a period demarcated by events. What we see as an age is only a deceptive reflection of a deeper reality, which is a coming into being. As we "age," we come into being in every moment.

To write a new translation for our age out of the urgency brought on by tension with the age gone by is to participate in that eternal leap into existence. Yet in practice translating is a difficult, irritating, unsatisfactory business in many ways. The translator, as a writer, tires of being bound by the original author's idiosyncrasies, limited by another's subject matter; and the constant compromise between the original and the target language is wearing on one's self-esteem. Yet one can also experience elation in the process. When I read a great poem aloud, I feel the power of the words as if I had created them; and in the same way, bringing a thought out of another language into powerful English can infuse me with the delight of re-creation.

Then, too, the translator is constantly finding things that have never appeared before. New meanings arise from the reworked soil of thought like lilies released from sleep after years trapped beneath hardpan. The translator says, "Aha!" and lives (for a moment) in the moment, fleetingly experiencing as much of the divine as some would say we are capable of knowing on this earth. This "eureka" moment of discovery we share with the other "re-searchers" of humankind, whether they plumb poetry or physics, art or astronomy; and it links us again with Swedenborg.

A translator also has the excitement of finding blossoms hidden in plain sight. One of the great Swedenborg translators, George Dole, was musing in an idle moment with a couple of other scholars on the title of one of Swedenborg's scientific works, *Oeconomia Regni Animalis.* The traditional translation, dating from the nineteenth century, is *Economy of the Animal Kingdom;* yet the work is a study of human physiology and psychology and has little to do with what we would think of as the animal kingdom, as opposed to the vegetable or mineral kingdom. In conjunction with his colleagues, Dole realized that a more accurate translation would be something like *Dynamics of the Soul's Domain*—that is, the interaction of elements of human physiology that lie under the control of the human soul. Each title is an equally plausible translation of the actual Latin words; yet in Dole's new version, the meaning suddenly springs to life.

These new meanings are intensely prolific. There is no telling what new translations can sow, what they can fertilize. And each refertilization, each sowing, has to happen anew in each age. John Keats wrote feelingly of the powerful experience of reading Chapman's translation of Homer's poetry—"Never did I breathe its pure serene/Till I heard Chapman speak out loud and bold." Yet today we would find Chapman's translation stifling. In the early part of the twentieth century, students in schools often read Palmer's translation of the *Odyssey,* a dreary rendering in nineteenth-century prose of Homer's epic. Robert Fitzgerald and Richmond Lattimore produced their fresh versions in the 1950s and 1960s, and suddenly students could breathe in Homer's age again. Some of those students went on in succeeding decades to write their own translations, tilling the spring soil again.

Some fear this new fertilization. I know of one high-school instructor who was confronted by an angry mother while he was teaching the *Odyssey* in Fitzgerald's translation. *That* was not Homer, she argued; she had her copy of Palmer in hand to prove it. That last of Palmer's fans, remarkably enough, had been able to see the realms of gold in Homer even when reading of them in that dry old translation. Her reaction is in a way understandable: we become attached to the translations that remind us of our first breath of spring. I myself have struggled in vain to like the translators of Homer who came after Lattimore, though when I consider them objectively I can see how they would appeal to students today. Perhaps in the same way the new translation of Swedenborg will require a new generation of readers.

The upshot of this is the paradoxical notion that in one sense the success of a translation can be measured by how quickly it is superseded. The group that has now come together to retranslate Swedenborg's works would in that respect like nothing better than to be superseded in turn; to see another new English Swedenborg spring into existence in the decades after our efforts are published.

I would like to say, "the group that has *begun to* come together to retranslate Swedenborg's works," because I hope there will be more who want to join this somewhat frail core of three, or four if I count myself. It is a testimony to Swedenborg's energy that it takes so many of us to render into English the work of only part of his lifetime, and that it requires the resources of an entire nonprofit foundation, with its many active volunteers and staff members, to support a publication project that he managed single-handedly. Of course, it is an axiom that the more people who are involved in an undertaking, the more difficult it becomes. Swedenborg at least had unanimity among his staff of one.

Nevertheless, the translators have proved, so far, remarkably unanimous, that they all want to produce readable English, not yet another dust-dry version. But achieving the simplicity of the Latin of Swedenborg's theological works is not an easy task. And these works, no matter how dry and cramped the old translations may make them appear, are startlingly simple in the original Latin. I had read them in the old translations first and was astonished when I turned to the Latin, not only by how readily understandable the original is, but at how emotionally accessible it remains even after two hundred years. The Latin descriptions of Swedenborg's experiences in the other world, as well as his earnest and lucid exposition of how we should live together in harmony in this world, are often deeply moving—life-shaking, one might say. One could compare it to the speech of angels, as described by Swedenborg himself:

> Because the speech of angels corresponds to their emotional basis, which is one of love, and because love in heaven means loving God and loving our neighbor, it is clear how elegant and pleasing their speech must be. It reaches not only the ears, but the inner depths of the minds of those who hear it.
>
> There was a certain hard-hearted spirit. An angel spoke with him; and by the angel's speech he was ultimately so affected that the tears flowed from him. He said that he could not restrain them; that love was speaking; and that he had never wept before. (*Heaven and Hell*, paragraph 238)

When I think of translating this "speech of angels," of bringing the profound emotional basis of Swedenborg's work into English along with the denotations of the words—sometimes I shake my head along with my friends at the boldness of the attempt.

In translating, my icon is the Swedenborg of Borges' poem: a man striding beside the angels, calling them by their secret names. When I reread a passage after translating, I test it against my image of that man. Would he approve? I try it by weighing its power, its ring, against the voice I have heard in the Latin. If I feel that emotional tingling, that whisper of the angel's language in the words, then I think that Swedenborg would be pleased. I think then that Swedenborg will be retilled and rise again from the earth, refreshed and vital in his new English verdure; that his age will find another springtime in ours.

Perhaps the new translations will succeed in conveying this emotional basis, and perhaps they will be only partially successful; perhaps it will remain for the next age to achieve this complete revivifying of the English text.

In the meantime, we are making at least this contribution: we are annotating the translations to explain the context in which Swedenborg's works arose so that readers can better understand the age from which he sprang. Even though he is often seen as a divinely inspired revelator, the terms in which he spoke were those he had acquired in very earthly study of Neo-Platonism, of science, and of the literature of his day.

The surprising thing is that seeing what *his* age was like, and what his part in it was, makes him that much more alive in *our* age. After all, we are all individuals living *in* an age, and living *out* a series of ages within our own lifetimes. The points at which these multiple ages connect or veer asunder are mapping points in our attempts to partake of our humanity; and these mapping points can be traced in relationships, in art, in learning, in all the myriad human endeavors we pursue. Each of the contributions in this volume of the Chrysalis Reader arises out of the tension between ages, between our own and others, or between our own era and other eras, other times. Each piece here shows us as human beings "rocking the ages"—pushing and pulling against the limitations of one age, seeking the freedom of another; retilling, refertilizing, remaking ourselves in the mirror of eternity, as Swedenborg would tell us we will one day remake ourselves in the world beyond.

STUART SHOTWELL *is a professional writer and editor who lives in Lubec, Maine, the easternmost point in the United States. He received his doctorate in classical philology in 1984 and now serves as the managing editor of the New Century Edition of the Works of Emanuel Swedenborg, forthcoming from the Swedenborg Foundation. He would like to acknowledge the support of Jonathan S. Rose, the series editor of the new translation, whose ideas on translating Swedenborg have been so inspirational that "it would be difficult in some cases," Dr. Shotwell says, "to remember that they were not originally my own."*

Rocking the Ages

THE PULSE OF CONTINUITY AND CHANGE

PART I

Between Worlds

ANDERS HALLENGREN

Rhythms of Repercussion
A Journey in Tommie Haglund's Musical Universe

THE LIGHTS LOWER IN THE ROCK nestling the Berwald Hall in Stockholm. It is 17 February 1995, and snowflakes are dancing in the winter evening. Sweden's Radio Music is presenting composer Tommie Haglund (b. 1959) in its modern music series. In the dusk quiet expectation spreads over the great mountain hall. There is a mood of solemnity. The celebrated poet Tomas Tranströmer, well-known for his dulcet metaphors, has traveled in to Stockholm to attend. Haglund's music has been played in England, Canada, the States, France, Morocco, Germany, Hungary, Austria, Iceland, and in all Scandinavian countries. Now it is meeting for the first time a larger Swedish audience.

Tommie Haglund studied with Sven-Eric Johanson (1919–1997). For both of them their meeting led to a deepening appreciation of Swedenborg's visionary world. Both have written musical works in honor of the mystic. For the 1988 Swedenborg tricentennial, three hundred years after the great man's birth, Haglund wrote *Intensio Animi*, a piece about the soul's intensity, about the power in the spirit's striving, and about immortality, inspired by central texts from Swedenborg.

On stage in the spotlight, the cellist John Ehde moves silently; behind him the pianist Carl-Axel Dominique bends ready over the keyboard, focusing intently on the notes. Suddenly the music's world opens, with a single, long tone. A scraping tone that transports my

Opposite:
Cycladic Marble Statuette: Harper.
III millenium B.C.
The Metropolitan Museum of Art, New York. Rogers Fund, 1947.

thoughts to the rasping of huge Tibetan *radong* brass instruments, tearing me back in time to the inspired poet Lena Måndotter's performance several evenings ago at Café 44, where she recited: "Travel to Kailash, the Holy Mountain." MAGIC THEATER—FOR MADMEN ONLY! a chimerical sign had announced to me outside. It was a quaint place, full of graffiti on the walls, cluttered, cold, shabby—best to keep the coat on. Commingling were several youngsters with shaved heads, looking like fighting; old men and women sitting lonely with their ale, among dashing theater-goers. A rhythmically swelling, deep-monotone hum from the loudspeakers hypnotically made the temperature rise.

"It was like climbing into a crack between two worlds," Lena recounts the long, long fevered dream she had while staying in a 6,000-meter-high mountain pass in the Trans-Himalayas. "But it can happen anywhere," she says, "it could happen in a staircase." She described her dream in a tone-poem:

> Here, at Tara's pass
> Under these intruding heavens
> On this precipice, something in me
> Called a meeting
> With what was wanting in me
>
> I follow the voice, which turns
> To you, your absence
> Here, in the innermost zone
>
> A voice, a rhythm, a movement
> A score of signs

The next note snatches me back to the hall at Berwald, and I journey further into Haglund's intuitive and visionary tone structure, where he seeks to find a way to man's inner being, to give expression to visions, to faint feelings, to give barrier-penetrating glimpses. But immediately complications and dissonances confront us. Disparate tones falling like icicles in desolate dreams, as if one took the front off a piano and plucked the strings, or the cat walked over the keyboard at random, musing. Now, sudden attacks—streaks of notes running in parallel, not classical but tonal, diaphanously oriental. Then wistful, romantic bow-strokes open out, arpeggios, weakly scraping echoes of sound—intimately seeking, listening. The piano seems to chase the cello, pursues it, frightens it; they chase each other like Tom and Jerry. New picture: John Ehde plays softly behind the bridge, right down near the support. Then everything is gone.

Immediately following this comes the premier performance of *Inim-inim,* a 1994 piece for violin and piano commissioned by the Swedish Radio. Violinist Dan Almgren has taken his place in front of Dominique. The title of the piece is Sumerian and expresses an invocation. 'Inim' means 'word', and here the composer approaches the lost prehistoric Word, the *Logos,* the founding Word in whose reverberation we live. Deep within this the composer seeks the key to the nature of reality. An incomprehensible piece about the inexpressible? It's easy to take the music as simply this, but the whole time new views open here. It begins quietly with romantic intimacy that is at once challenged by chaotic piano; there is an oscillation between chaos and harmony without rest, perpetual change, the violinist flays, the word 'keys' has lost its meaning. Then suddenly one realizes that the piano is the Law, the violin man's budding raw Will. A landscape opens. Silent raindrops fall on the snow, patches of mist rise, and in the distance there's a song. The undefined confusion is opposed by the persistent piano, progressively maintaining and emphasizing harmony while an ensemble of sound gradually develops, almost in unison. But then everything slides by and ends in an obviously wrong note: an open question.

More accessible but also full of depth is *Speglingar [Reflections],* a 1993 piece for coloratura soprano, violin, cello, and piano. It was written for the American singer Janet Chvatal, and here this evening it is Tua Åberg who is the center of the swirl of sound. The piece's title reflects Swedenborg's thoughts on the correspondence between spiritual and material things, between earthly and heavenly worlds, and that every truth is a mirror of other truths. Even the composer's early interest in both astronomy and music comes in here. All these earlier elements have been poured together into this piece: the playing of the violin and cello mirrors the bell-clear soprano. The tones of sacramental music come forth, the ringing sounds of the Middle Ages pour out, enormously deep. A wonderful light floods into the soul's dark night. Souls reflect each other in themselves.

THE ENSEMBLE'S PERFORMERS CONCLUDE the evening's portrait of the composer at the Opera Cellar restaurant. I have at my table Monica Dominique and the artist Soldanella Oyler. Carl-Axel Dominique offers a toast to both Haglund and Swedenborg, and after a moment recalls Verner von Heidenstam's book *Svenskarna och deras hövdingar [Swedes and Their Leaders],* where a story is told of Swedenborg inviting a spirit to have meatballs with him at the table in his garden. Carl-Axel's thoughts go further to the composer Bo Nilsson and the artist Carl Frederick Reuterswärd, who made an absurd surrealistic TV-film on Swedenborg, where the clown Beppo enters the scene. After a few minutes Carl-Axel Dominique shifts his focus again and attempts to describe something of the nature of music and his own role in this. "I believe music can express thinking.

What Wittgenstein says about language setting the boundaries of thought is all wrong! There's thought in music, too. Even the graphic arts are bound more to visible reality: music is the unseen reality."

Everyone seems to feel in tune with the evening. Tommie Haglund is happy. Monica Dominique talks about the interplay between the musician and the audience, how the experience grows through those who are there. "But even the birds are musicians," Carl-Axel chimes in. "Music isn't made just by people." There's music in nature, he thinks, giving as an example the fact that the ornithologist Eric Rosenberg has written down songs of birds with their notes. And then he calls to mind the connection of musical thought with my Emerson studies—Charles Ives and his piano sonata, *Concord, Massachusetts*. Dominique is familiar with this piece because he played it at his first major concert appearance. Ives sought to express Emerson's thinking in his music, to summarize the contents of Emerson's essays.

At the Underground Waters

IT'S SUMMER. The sun is shining warmly over Lummelunda's chalk formations outside Visby on the island of Gotland, formed by animals in a prehistoric sea. Beneath the ground stretches a four-hundred-million-year-old coral reef. Led by a group of cave explorers, wading and scrambling I have crept on hands and knees into the inner cold of these remarkable grottos. We have passed "The Skerry," "The Clay Harbor," "The Square," "The Sand Bank," and "Horseback Sea", and now stop after a few hours in Tunnel 1 at the Siphon, the underwater entrance to "Ship's Hall." We sit along the walls covered with clay. Small black shrimps glide out into the water across the bottom, far from the light of day and the sea. Here the underground water life still goes on: like blind spiders weaving their webs, fish wander about unconcerned by the darkness. We muddy the lamps on our foreheads as we douse them, switch them off. We rest in the darkness surrounded by silence deep inside the mountain massif, a blackness and quiet without end in the rooms of fossils from a past time, dead beings who have become stone. Only distant drippings now and then ring and echo. Timelessness expands itself into a general intermission of the water symphony. *The Tibetan Book of the Dead!*

In the middle period after death, the light of dusk prevails, one is squeezed into tunnels of frighteningly strange emptiness and quiet, plaguing images, the opening of new possibilities, rebirth's hopes and fears. Alone one wanders through the grottoes; this is the *Bardo* state, where one must stay clear of the exits. Nothing is certain. Forced into submission, pressed and squeezed by rocks and stones, the wanderer becomes aware of being near a new womb. Released once again, emptiness spreads itself, the emptiness of nothingness. One's senses are on edge, assaulted by pictures and sounds; reality thunders in memory's echoes. One doesn't see one's image mirrored in the water. At the crossroads of decision one senses that there are paths going in different directions, up and down. Dreams, reflections, reverberations—the ocean of suffering is not far off. From holes in the earth, from tunnels and chambers, fear wells up and hits one in the face. The most dangerous thing is the exit. "Don't be afraid," Death's guide says, "life is the easiest refuge." There in the darkness you seem to be falling through an abyss into the wasteland of loneliness and silence. Follow the narrow way toward the light! Through snow, rain, wind, and darkness, for the one listening, waiting for eternity, the holy words and tones reverberate throughout the world. One hears distant drippings through the mountain.

Speleology and deep psychology! For many years the *Bardo Tödol* was Carl Gustav Jung's constant companion. He wrote an analytic commentary on this Book of the Dead, which was published as a foreword in the German and English editions. Jung focused on the traumatic element in the birth to new life that his teacher Freud had brooded over. But he went a step further, to the trauma of death and rebirth. He found the agreements with Swedenborg's reports about the state of transition at death remarkable, namely, that in the beginning the person who has died does not know he is dead, that life is continuing. The fact that Swedenborg echoes the insights of the Tibetans, Jung attributed to a timeless level within us that crosses all boundaries, the *collective unconscious*. Swedenborg's case shows this, he thought. To this add the tunnel experience, and the light breaking through at its end. *The Tibetan Book of the Dead* is a closed book that can be opened only by initiation and experience, Jung says.

In your wandering, the *Book* reports further, your body appears in the color of the light toward which you are wandering. The yellow light of mankind's world and the smoke-colored light of the underworld clash against the shimmering white clarity of the worlds of the gods, or the gleaming blue and green of the various spirit worlds. There is a whole spectrum here, where one is drawn in a particular direction according to one's inner affinity. Such is the route one takes on the Other Side.

Every mood, every attitude, has a tone, a color. This is a general symbolism in hermetic traditions from ancient times to our own. Even Newton saw the connection between art and music, color and sound, hearing and seeing. In one of his notebooks at Cambridge he attempted, using logarithms, to give mathematical expression to eighteen different keys, Chinese as well as Greek. He, the researcher of light, experienced the analogy between the seven colors of the spectrum of light and the seven-tone scale.

Thus, the scale of the normal tones was reflected in the universe; or rather the other way around, the cosmos is the basis for music on earth. All the Western world's thinking about music can be found in journeys through worlds beyond, such as in Pythagorean mathematics: the doctrine of the universe's music. "We are all Pythagoreans," says the modern composer Iannis Xenakis. The statement applies to Stockhausen and Hindemith. The most modern of the moderns, serialists in tune with Milton Babbit and Pierre Boulez, have closed the circle in their turning back to thousand-year-old traditions, seeking the cosmic harmony and outer-space's echoes of chaos, as well as the background noise of the moment of creation in the distance; the spatial world's laws and intervals; or the mathematics of heaven, as in Pythagoras' Babylonian–Sumerian mystical interpretation of numbers. This cycle of music history has been finely described by Jamie James in his book *The Music of the Spheres* (London: Abacus, 1995). Music has meaning because the universe has a meaning. Its tones are a language, as are feelings and nature-elements in the text of reality.

Like many others who have gone back to the mystical element in the tradition of classical music, Haglund, like Sven-Eric Johanson, has experimented with tonal series and permutations. Then abandoning this he has chosen to seek his own way. But in the end intuitively created music always shows itself to possess a strong inner structure, Haglund says. For him, music is often a rite of initiation, a process of transition. The spirit is totally sacral. With this end in view the Grand Theme is again referred to—healing and purification and revelation, all in harmony with the universe—an opening to another world. It is a music with purport and purpose, and it has a vital mission: spiritual development. This is music's function, its *usus*—its "use," one of Swedenborg's central terms. It is not an end in itself or art for art's sake. We shall see later how this thought recurs in Haglund's work for Save the Children. For children, he says, music is a preparation for life, an important part in the developmental process. And it can also be a preparation for death. But there are no distinct paths here, one must find and choose them for oneself—and it is in this striving that music can elevate us.

Haglund summarizes his attraction to Swedenborg: "Where your love is on earth, there you will come on the other side. There is no god who casts you into hell—this message appeals to me." And here Swedenborg, in concord with *The Tibetan Book of the Dead*, gives us a glimpse of this other world: a vision Haglund feels is the innermost essence of composing. To rightly see the constellation

Vincent van Gogh. *The Starry Night.* Oil on canvas, 29×36¼ inches, 1889. The Museum of Modern Art, New York. Acquired through the Lillie P. Bliss Bequest. Photograph ©2000 The Museum of Modern Art, New York.

Haglund–Swedenborg, where music, science, and the mystical can be conceived of as different sides of the same thing, we must direct our sight to the starry heaven of older music theory.

The Myth of Er, Scipio's Dream, and the Vision of Timarchos

THE LATE ROMAN AUTHOR BOETHIUS is best known for his wonderful essay *The Consolation of Philosophy*, written in 524 when he sat imprisoned awaiting his execution. Another of his writings that was read all through the Middle Ages is *De Institutione Musica*. In this fragmentary and incomplete work he summarized and systematized the musical theory of the ancient Pythagorean tradition. In the spirit of Pythagoras and Ptolemy he made visible music's three interwoven worlds: *musica instrumentalis*, *musica humana* [the harmony of soul and body] and *musica mundana* [the cosmic harmony].

At a certain moment these worlds can sound together in harmony, and therein lies a powerful force. Music can set the human mind in a universal direction: the connection between body and soul can be tuned to the laws of the universe. For this reason, according to this tradition, there is also a significant healing power in music. The quick rise of interest in music therapy in the later part of the twentieth century is a resumption of this ancient tradition. Music is not simply medicine for the soul; it is also an ethical knowledge, a way to know the inner laws of life and the universe. All knowledge goes into music.

In the *quadrivium,* the "fourfold way" of the classical school, music is set on the same level as the other pillars of knowledge: arithmetic, geometry, and astronomy. One cannot come further from the idea of music as entertainment. Music is knowledge, in its perfect form an expression of the universe.

With Boethius, as with Pythagoras and Swedenborg and Haglund, musical thought rests on mystical experience, on the visionary, on journeys into the inner spaces. One can sense the enormous breadth and significance of this tradition in Plato as well as in Cicero and Plutarch. Against the background of visions these authors have written down to make what has been said clear, both Haglund's and Swedenborg's worlds fit into a larger pattern, a pattern where distinct pictures stand out as reflections, or variations on the same theme. I have in mind the Myth of Er, Scipio's Dream, and Timarchos' Vision. Here all boundaries—limits such as geography and history, space and time—are erased between faith and knowledge, the humanities and science.

In the last book of Plato's dialogue *The State* (*Politeia,* §X:614b–619b) Socrates recounts the Myth of Er. It is a description that anticipates Dante and Swedenborg. It is a retelling of a near-death experience. This description concludes and summarizes a dialogue whose subject is the nature of justice. The perspective is raised from a consideration of the individual's and the state's concept of justice to a vision of cosmic justice. The good and the evil befall their appointed places and fated destiny. The world on the other side has a fixed and established order, like the order of outer space. The heavens sing of the harmony of the divine law. Plato writes,

> I will tell the story of a brave man named Er, a son of Armenius, who was among the many warriors killed in a pitched battle. On the ninth day when the dead were carried off, his body was found well preserved among the wounded and decaying corpses. He was carried home and on the twelfth day; when he was to be cremated, he suddenly got up from the pyre. As he revived, he related what he had experienced in the other state. He said that after his soul had left his body, it journeyed together with many others to a spiritual place, where there were two openings beside each other in the earth, and two openings above in the heavens.

Between these one meets judges, who after a conversation indicate the right direction to go. But these guiding spirits in the middle state appoint Er to be a messenger between the worlds and urge him to make careful observations and then return and report them.

Er meets with souls going on distant journeys in many directions. He learns that after they come to the fork in the road after death they are on a thousand-year journey, upwards through the first opening or downwards through the first breach into the underworld; they at last return through the second openings to travel further to the throne of Necessity, to a distribution of Fate's lots and new bodily shapes—and then they drink from the Cup of Forgetfulness and return to earth.

The only thing souls can vaguely remember are the eternal laws that prevail in the world back on the other side. Earthly concepts like those of Justice, Goodness, and Beauty are reminiscences of this kind.

Heaven's concord and order make Er feel giddy, but so also does learning the fate of souls, and he tells stories that carry one's thoughts to the memorabilia of Swedenborg's spiritual experiences. He sees famous men and women and a train of tyrants pass in review. To no one is it given to wriggle out of fate's grip and escape his destined due. Er wonders how it had gone with king Ardiaios from his home tract of Pamphylia, a tyrant who at one point in time had murdered his father and his brother. "He never comes to us here," his countrymen in heaven report.

> Then we saw something quite remarkable play itself out before us. When we were near the entrance to the tunnel, and were in the process of ascending after a great deal of effort, we suddenly saw both him and others. Most of them were kings, but there were ordinary people too who had committed terrible crimes. They were standing as if waiting to climb upwards—but just at that moment the tunnel's mouth in front of them would close.
>
> He added that after they themselves had spent seven days in the land of shadow, they had to break up on the eighth day and in the next four days make a trip to another place. There they were given to see a light stretching like a pillar between heaven and earth, resembling a rainbow but clearer and more glorious. This is the center of the worlds, from which the mighty circular movements of the cosmos spread themselves, one after the other, ring after ring, and all have a color and a tone. The seventh has the strongest light, and the eighth takes its color from the light of the seventh, the second and the fifth are like each other, but are yellower than the others. The third has the whitest color, the fourth is the reddest [...] and-on every circle there was a Siren in the whirling who sang out with a sound, a tone, and the eight sounded together in a symphonic harmony [... *harmonían symphoneîn*].

The myth of Er has been understood as a musical allegory, and it is easy to find the seven-tone scale with the octave as the eighth tone, like finding the twelve tones of the half-tone scale in the colossal cosmology of the *Timaios*—where the intervals are carefully reckoned, together with their "manifold correspondences"—harmonic chords in fourths and fifths, like the inward dissonances between these. This is the harmony of the spheres, music's world of ideas, which holds within itself even chromatic tension, a primeval sea of music that would sound cacophonic if it were to fall into the world of our senses in its entirety. But the point in Socrates' account that Plato transcribes is that the ideal state—like Music in its perfection, as the Good of Life and the Beautiful—rests on cosmic laws.

It is for this reason that one finds a similar description in Cicero, the Roman philosopher of law, in the seventh part of his book on the state, *De re publica*. It is Scipio's Dream.

This piece of the original, now lost manuscript, has been saved for posterity thanks to its being quoted a half-thousand years later in the commentary to *Somnium Scipionis [The Dream of Scipio]* taken down by the learned manuscript collector Macrobius. In this way this remarkable account of astral music has echoed through the writings of countless later authors.

In a dream, Scipio Africanus minor meets his grandfather Scipio Africanus major and is introduced into the world where the dead reside: The Milky Way, the Galaxy, where a vivid circle of enrapturing clarity is found in the starry heaven.

> I stood dumfounded before this scene, and, when I came to my senses, I asked, 'What is that wonderful sound filling my ears?' My grandfather answered: 'That is the harmony of tones separated by different great but carefully tuned intervals created by the rapid movement of the spheres [...] different tones that one can say are the key to the whole universe. By imitating these tones on string instruments and in song, gifted men have created a connection with this region [...] The ears of the mortals are filled with this music, but they cannot hear it.'

Finally, in Plutarch's philosophic work *Moralia* (§ 590 a–c), which treats of a number of subjects, among them music, we find Timarchos' Vision. It comes up in a dialogue on Socrates' *daimonion,* one's inner voice or guardian spirit, one's moral conscience. Simmias, leader of the conspiracy that had just freed Thebes from the Spartans' grip, reports:

> Timarchos, who wanted to learn about the nature of the daimonion, set about this as the philosophically initiated young man that he was. After taking counsel with Cebes as well as me, he descended into Trophonius' chasm, observing all the oracle's customary rituals. He remained under the earth two days and two nights, and by this time most of the people had given up hope that he would ever return; his family mourned him as dead. But then at daybreak he came up, his face gleaming. He prayed to God and then, as soon as the crowd had gone, told of the remarkable things he had heard and seen.
>
> He said that the first thing he experienced after climbing down into the oracle's crypt was great darkness. He said a prayer and then lay for a long time, uncertain whether he was awake or dreaming. [...] When he lifted up his eyes the earth was nowhere to be seen, but he saw islands that lit up each other with a soft, fiery light, one after the other, the light changing with their movements. They appeared to be countless in number and huge in size, and although they were all different, they were all round, and he imagined that it was their circular movements that produced the musical sound that spread itself in the ether,

because the pleasant sound that arose as harmony between the different tones corresponded to the rhythm of the movements.

Far in the distance behind Er, Scipio, and Timarchos one senses the presence of the legendary Orpheus, who with his lyre in his hand could exert control over creation itself and make the underworld open; and where he traveled to get his beloved Eurydice from the world of the dead. In the myth of Er, the oldest of the above cited accounts, Plato scholars (among them Johann Matthias Gesner in Swedenborg's time and, more recently, Francis Macdonald Cornford) have thought they glimpsed remnants of older accounts in the Orphic and Pythagorean traditions. The central point is the doctrine of music's universality and divine nature. It is no coincidence that—more than two thousand years later—opera was born under the sign of Orpheus. The early Italian operas—Giulio Romano Caccini's *Euridice,* Jacopo Peri's *Euridice,* and Claudio Monteverdi's *Orfeo,* all treated of Orpheus—of music's boundary-breaking power.

The old Greek tradition tells of music's compelling power, its ability to tame the wildest beasts, to pour oil on the waves, to inspire to battle, or to healing faith, to actually rise from the dead. A powerful center in this tradition is the mathematician and cosmologist Pythagoras in the sixth century BC, and his secret brotherhood of followers through the ages. In his biography of Pythagoras, Iamblichos from Chalkis tells us of a young man in Taormina, Sicily. This young man had partied the whole evening with friends to music in the Phrygian key, which was known to excite aggressiveness. In the morning hours, when he saw his beloved slinking out of the house of his rival, he decided to burn her house down. Pythagoras, who himself had been out that night studying the stars, became aware of what was about to happen. He then got the night's musicians to change note and perform a song in spondees, a calming metre, and in this way warded off the catastrophe. Pythagoreans, Iamblichos reports, had a special music to get to sleep, another for awakening, and healed diseases in this way. The flutist and the cosmos can play on the same note.

Boethius' Christian colleague at Theoderic the Great's court, the humanist Cassiodorus (c. 480–580), had also emphasized music's universal content in his great work *Institutiones.* The universe is created and governed by music. "If we live virtuously, we are under its influence. If we sin, we lack music."

Music during the Renaissance and Baroque periods grew from the same thinking. Renaissance hermeticism instituted musical home-remedies of the kind that is coming back again in our days—in handbooks like Hal A. Lingerman's *The Healing Energies of Music*

Gustav Klimt.
Die Musik I [Music I].
Bayerische
Staatsgemäldesammlungen,
Neue Pinakothek,
Munich.

(1983). According to this living tradition, music is a medium for cosmic energies, which can be used here on earth. The widely influential Platonic and hermetic philosopher Marsilio Ficino (1433–1499) composed a book about a life of a heavenly nature, *De vita cœlitus comparanda,* that was a guide to using music for self-improvement and development, where he even examined disharmonies, evil influences, and dangers. Swedenborg's strange reports from the Moon and the planets in our solar system (*De Telluribus,* 1758) completely lack astronomical content but should be understood against the background of Ficino and the Hermetic tradition's astrology. It is different states of mind and moods that are described in the pictures from the seer's inner journeys, different aspects of the Greatest Man, *maximus homo,* who is heaven; and this is the book's subject, as is evident from its introduction. In this journey, angelic choirs break in, singing *qui simul una voce et cùm concentu* [as with one voice and in harmony].

Musica humana, the music that plays in body and soul, can be tuned in universal harmony. It is thus that our situation is presented also in the first oratorio, Emilio de' Cavalieri's mystery play *Rappresentazione di anima e di corpo* (1600), as in Emanuel Swedenborg's philosophical essay *De commercio animae et corporis* (1769) and in other works.

The break between this older time and our own, happens in Romanticism's subjectivization and the dissolution of all hierarchies in the course of the nineteenth century. Then the old picture of the world fell. The breakthrough of modern times was the breaking-up of a several-thousand-years-old tradition, a cut in time. How near in time and thought we still stand to this older and now unknown world is what I have here wanted to bring to mind. Tommie Haglund stands between two worlds, in between two musical traditions. His sensitivity, his conception of music as "the outburst of the soul" is partially romantic. But in the same high degree it has its roots in the baroque world of affections, as described in, for instance, Athanasius Kircher's *Musurgia universalis* (1650): the doctrine of the affections, according to which it is music's task "to illustrate and imitate different emotional states." It is against this background that the oldest opera, as well as Bach's vocal works and Handel's oratorios, are played.

L'Estate—Summer. Eternal Movement

I CALL TOMMIE HAGLUND in July 1995. Grotto safari in Lummelunda, of which I am telling him, has a strong appeal for him as a musical experience: to hear that silence. He himself is sitting in his house in Eldsberga outside Halmstad on the Swedish west coast and is writing a cello concert commissioned by the National Concerts. Its source of inspiration: tones from our planets' journey through the universe in a recording made by the American space program, *Songs of Earth* (NASA Space Probe Recordings, 1991). To this remarkable Pythagorean harmony, now heard by radio-astronomy, he is adding strokes of overtones.

Besides this, together with fiancée Elisabet Löfberg, he is producing a book and CD commissioned by the Swedish Save the Children Fund, that is intended for use by personnel at day-care centers and pre-schools, and by others who are engaged in children's development. They are working with Assistant Professor Kristoffer Konarski at the Karolinska Institute in Stockholm on a project in which the brain specialist Professor David Ingvar has assisted with advice. The project's purpose is to strengthen the emotional development of children through music. Music is seen as a firm foundation for harmonic development: "What one cannot come to in children through words one approaches using musical expression, opening visions and other worlds," Tommie explains. One is born with the ability to have feelings, but one does not have them from the beginning. It is here, he means, that music can be an aid. He sees deficient emotional development as the great threat in a world of continual changes and new situations, where rich emotional development is the only thing that can hinder aimlessness, chaos, and indifferent action.

"Making right choices requires emotional tools," he continues. "A person is born with two fundamental feelings that are very broad concepts, pain and a sense of well-being; and some people come no further in their development, swinging between these two conditions like a small child." These two fundamental feelings have their origin in two perceptions during the fetal state, the perceptions of two tempos: *fast* and *slow*. When the rhythm of the mother's heart is calm and content with existence, the blood pulsates more slowly and softly in the body. When she is stressed or experiences something unpleasant, it goes more quickly. One has no feelings in the fetal state; there is no sorrow, anger, or anxiety—it is the above two perceptions that set the tone. From these the two fundamental feelings are developed: from the hurried, grow anger and pain; in the slow paced are formed experiences of well-being, rest, and timelessness. Before there is speech and language, these states in the infant develop into anger, joy, sorrow, and unrest; and in its emotional development the content of these feelings must be made conscious. One must learn about them and make contact with them in order to understand oneself and one's environment and be able to act harmoniously with others. Many, both children and adults who have deficiencies in this development, can react with wrong feelings and in wrong situations. Even feelings are a language. Sympathy develops of itself when there is a functioning inward and outward interplay of the other feelings. All feelings have a life-preserving function; this is why we have them.

> *What does music express?* I asked Haglund.
>
> An emotional outburst from the soul—it can be quiet, it can be explosive, but the soul of music is more like this than an expression of theories or mathematical formulas. At the same time it is not merely a series of feelings that stream fourth without structure; it has a form with an inner pattern and coherence.

Music can also be contemplation, an attempt to reach an inner reality in meditation. Therein lies its spiritual breadth. Haglund uses sounds to attain this mood, to generate this state, to find the points in the world of vibrations most touchingly rich with emotion. Before he begins a piece of music he has a mood clearly in mind, a vision: "I see clear pictures before me." While he is in deep repose, these musically charged scenes, the font of his music, pass before him. When he wrote a piece for soprano he was sitting in his workroom and suddenly saw the whole view outside go dark.

> The forest and everything was completely black and the sky had assumed the color of silver. Then suddenly a yellow rock rose up out of the earth and a lightening flashed out of the rock, and there was a face on the rock looking on. It was a frighteningly strong experience [...] Behind the picture is music.

One night he was wakened by hearing a soprano. At that moment he had been about to go into a church in his dream. He was held back, and then suddenly everything collapsed. But the songstress continued to sing, the sun shone in, and in the middle among all the illuminated blocks of stone stood a baby carriage. These pictures—of the same kind as those images Salvador Dalí always saw before he put his brush to the canvas—he tries to retain as long as needed to get into their music. And the music produces pictures. "What kind of music a person likes depends on the situation, on the wave-length a person is on just then; you can't talk about a 'favorite piece' or 'the best music'." Haglund talks about openness, to those involved in the education of children, too: "Sitting as if you were in front of an open fire, simply letting yourself be fascinated by the sparks it throws off now and then, although you don't know when it's going to happen,...." Depending on how one grew up, some people have an easier time of finding certain wavelengths than others. Behind music lies experience, life. In music a person enters into life, and goes further.

> What fascinates me most in Swedenborg is that he saw so clearly into another world and still could act normally. Without making other comparisons, I have nothing more to say than that music is my way of seeing into another world. Here the spirit-seer and the composer meet. It is important to dare to let go of theories and formulas: they lie like blocks in the path of concentration.

"What is the connection between music and religion?" I ask.

> You can come into a church and the music elevates everything. But it is the spirit of fellowship in church that is the essential element in the worship, and this is what is the center in music, too. Its base is the very experience itself, and the tones reach beyond the words. In music one can come near to the Divine.

The now deceased teacher Sven-Eric Johanson was on the same wavelength. His significance consisted mostly in his support. In July 1995, when he heard *Inim-inim* and *Reflections,* he sat in his wheelchair and appeared to see into another world; sometimes their eyes met. Afterwards he took Tommie Haglund's hands and squeezed them hard. No words were necessary. It was often so. They shared a spiritual dimension. The first thing they talked about when they first met was music's spirituality; it was the Whitman-inspired Frederick Delius (1862–1934) who brought them together. Haglund was going to write an article about Delius in *Kvällsposten [The Evening Post].* He then wanted to have a comment about his music from a composer and knew that Johanson usually included Delius' *Requiem* in his lectures. So it was that they began their long dialogue, and soon they were reading and discussing Swedenborg together, especially since Haglund had gone on to find Theodore Pitcairn's book *My Lord and My God* (1967). And thus they both found their way to Swedenborgian services of worship.

The work commissioned for the Swedenborg jubilee in 1988, *Intensio Animi*, was performed in November of that year in the Grünewald Hall in Stockholm's Concert House. Later Sven-Eric Johanson's tone-poem to Swedenborg was presented at The House of Culture, also in Stockholm. Haglund has a remarkable story to tell of how his own work came into being.

> I had just begun work on this piece when I visited the Strindberg Museum and caught sight of a costume poster for Strindberg's *The Black Glove* made by Charles Koroly, an English artist living in Sweden and working at the Royal Dramatic Theater. The picture etched a deep impression. It resembled Soldanella Oyler (b. 1913), and my piece is dedicated to her too. She was the one who introduced me to Swedenborg. She is fantastic. Her ancestors in direct descent were friends of Beethoven and Haydn. Her ancestor the composer Per Frigel (1750–1842), secretary of the Royal Academy of Music, arranged a stipend for Beethoven from the Academy.

Frigel, who had originally been called Frigelius but was renamed by his employer King Gustav III, figures as does Swedenborg himself in Bernhard von Beskow's *Recollections*. Haydn has dedicated a symphony to Frigel. The artist Soldanella Oyler is related to Conan Doyle and was in contact with the composer Hugo Alfvén and the author Verner von Heidenstam. Her mother, Elsa Giöbel Oyler (1882–1979), was also an artist and a Swedenborgian and knew the famous artist Carl Larson. Soldanella lived in Grez-sur-Loing as did Frederick Delius.

> I have been strongly inspired by Delius; he was the one who got me to composing. When I was studying guitar in London, I heard his music for the first time and got a shock. Then I made my decision. Delius was blind and lame during his last fifteen years when he lived in France. Then Eric Fenby, a young Englishman, came and offered to help him. The year was 1927, and this Englishman went on to become engaged to Soldanella, whom he also met in Grez-sur-Loing. Several books have been written about the collaboration that followed between Fenby and Delius—about how thirty-two-voice works were taken down by dictation. Ken Russell has made a movie about this. I met this remarkable Englishman when he was more than eighty years old. Fenby talked only about Soldanella, whom I didn't know at all. When I had come back to Sweden, she telephoned me; he had written a letter about my visit.
>
> She talked a long time about her meetings with Delius. I told her about my own visions, and then she mentioned Emanuel Swedenborg. It was 1986. Then my seeking came to fruition, at least to a certain extent. I traveled to Nora, where Soldanella lived. She had Theodore Pitcairn's book. It struck me as a lightning bolt. I accompanied her to a Swedenborgian worship service.
>
> To return to the poster: along with all this I had begun to compose, and the work led to *Intensio Animi*. I had begun to compose a solo piece for cello, which John Ehde had asked me to do, but then I saw that poster in the Strindberg Museum! I couldn't let go of it—not for a moment. When I got home I called the Strindberg Museum and wondered if I could buy a copy of it. But they told me that there was none.
>
> "It's a costume poster and this original is the only one there is. But you can call Charles Koroly and ask him," they said.
>
> I did. He wondered: "Why do *you* want *this?*"

I said that I was in process of doing a work for Emanuel Swedenborg's three-hundred-year anniversary and had seen this picture and that I felt it fitted the music inexpressibly. Then he said: "This is really remarkable, because I had Swedenborg in mind when I made it, all the time." Then he said he would make a copy.

Since then it has been hanging in my work room. I see it all the time. It's a woman in a black dress, and she looks as if she feels sorrow and is going away from something.

"How did this take you further in your music?" I asked.

This picture, it opened up sounds. It guided me like a lighthouse.

"Going on to Inim-inim," *I said.* *"What was the starting point?"*

The Rosicrucian Order has published a book entitled *From the Depth of Your Inner Being* which contains a chapter on the lost Word: a tone, a sound has set creation in motion, and this teaching about the lost Word is found in many early religions. 'Inim' in Sumerian means 'word', and *inim-inim* is an incantation. 'Inim' in Turkish means 'suffering'.

"Were you thinking of that too, of suffering?"

Yes, in a certain way. I was thinking that the suffering here on earth must have something to do with creation, too—something one must go through.

Our conversation is interrupted by a rhythmic crackling, in Morse code as it were. It's the farmer's electric fence outside, perhaps some creature has just now got too close. There, around this house called the "Paradise Apple House" outside Halmstad, cows are moving about in the pasture, grazing.

Within the house, in a separate workroom, at night in the composer's head, music is created. The hour is late before it's fixed on paper.

I write nothing down until everything's clear. It's a painful process. I'm trying to create a three-dimensional model, music rich in sound with several levels, with an inner structure. But I'm ignoring all conventions, everything that's taught, all the technical rules of composition. I'm following no textbooks, paying no attention to what any teacher says. *Inim-inim* begins on a B^b. A long series of trills strive toward B. It often tumbles over, tensions are created, but then at the end it becomes evident that this is not what was being searched for. The solution comes from another side, the whole piece comes down on an A, an enormous release! It's almost as if you look in a different direction and so see something totally new! It ends there, but it could just as well continue! I'm into the next piece! There are questions here that remain, questions that lead on.

"Finally, coming to Reflections [Speglingar], *what did you see before you?"*

It's tremendously romantic! My Elisabet, whom I share my life with, we've often said we reflect each other. It happens when we look in each other's eyes. There's actually a story that says that it's not just my own reflections that do this, but that everyone has this kind of relation to the world around him, more or less. A person has this kind of relation to some friends too. There's something in us where we reflect each other, we're each other's resonance. At the time I wrote the piece I also had a great sorrow. *Reflections* is a piece that contains the most romantic elements of all three; it's also the most tonal and harmonic.

> "There is a closeness to thousand-year-old musical traditions that press in here and there. Perhaps a search in the classical tradition's Great Theme, the harmony of the spheres?"

I got to know a French music researcher named Henri Corbeille, a specialist in Debussy, Ravel, and Delius. It was when we were living in Grez-sur-Loing. Corbeille was an old friend of Eric Fenby. When Corbeille heard *Reflections*, he said that he felt like a Hindu. This is precisely the thousand-year-old tradition you are talking about; it's the same thing. It is present in *Inim-inim*'s primeval presentiments. Just like you, many have felt themselves transported to Tibet at the opening of the *Intensio Animi*.

Thus in a wonderful way here are met with, in this music, the transcendental visions C.G. Jung noted in both Swedenborg and in *The Tibetan Book of the Dead*.

With yet another outburst of the strange rhythms of the farmer's fence, the rasping of which mutes our voices, we at last say good-byes. The hour is late, and we have already passed the limits of our talk and of this essay. The sky is high, and there is still a distant lowing of the cattle which are grazing on the hills. In a while Tommie Haglund closes the door behind him and sits down in his silent music room in the darkness, gazing into the night, waiting. The watchman says: "The morning cometh, and also the night: if ye will inquire, inquire ye: return, come."

ANDERS HALLENGREN is a professor in the Department of Literature and the History of Ideas at Stockholm University. Dr. Hallengren is also a project director of the Nobel Foundation and managing editor of *Parnass: The Journal of the Swedish Literary Societies*. Text of this article was translated from the original Swedish by Kurt Nemitz. A musical portrait of the composer, Tommie Haglund—*Inim-Inim*, has been issued and internationally released by the recording company Caprice (CAP 21522) 1998.

ARLENE DISTLER

For Alan at Fifty-three

After speaking of the haunting
cry of the hump-backed whale,
he lay in my arms—we two long-mated
on the couch, the mood melancholy.
I've just read of the pilot whale,
their grounding on Cape Cod's shore.

I hold him the way marine rescuers
cradle their out-sized waifs
to save them from themselves . . .
his sadness heavy, profound.
I know by its echo
its depth and weight.
The way astronomers know
a dense star
or a planet by its pull
on a neighboring body.

He wakes at night
uttering the sounds of nightmares,
watches the dance of dolphins
on TV, envies their ease.
He is trying to find his way
back to water.

ARLENE DISTLER is a poet, a painter, and mother of four. A featured reader in Vermont and Massachusetts, she has recorded her poetry for a series that aired on Vermont radio. She serves on several town boards. Her work has appeared in the *Seeing through Symbols* issue of the Chrysalis Reader, in two anthologies of women's writing: *Weaving Our Voices* and *Freedom's Just Another Word,* and in *Kalliope.*

PAMELA MAYER

When the Princess Died

ONCE A KING AND QUEEN's beautiful little daughter fell into the millpond and drowned. The King was grieving, and the Queen was grieving, and the whole palace was grieving. The King and the Queen were so sad they forgot all about ruling the Kingdom, and the folk in the palace were so sad they forgot to attend to their duties. The whole countryside was grieving as well. Black flags flew in all the towns, and before long the country folk were so sad they stopped bringing their goods into market, and the townspeople were so sad they stopped trading and buying. After a while the fish stopped rising in the ponds and the animals stopped giving birth in the barns, and after still another while, even the corn stopped growing in the fields.

One day the King's grandmother (a very old lady who lived in her own quarters in the north tower) rapped on the floor with her stick. The servant who attended her came running. "Fetch the King to speak with me," she commanded—and the fellow ran to do as he was told.

The King sighed and made his way through the long corridors to the north tower. "Good morning, Grandmother," he said respectfully.

"It's not good and you know it, Grandson," she snapped. "What's this about the fish not rising and the animals not giving birth and the corn not growing?"

"It's all because the Princess has died," said the King sadly.

Opposite:
Louise Nevelson.
Orfeo–Thrones.
Sculpture, gold leaf on wood, 1984.
Farnsworth Art Museum, Rockland, Maine. Gift of Louise Nevelson, 1985. Gift of the artist, 1991.

"Nonsense," said the old lady. "It's because you're selfish, and you've forgotten you're the King. Your grandfather wouldn't have behaved this way and neither would your father. I won't have it."

"But Grandmother . . ." began the King.

"Don't grandmother me," said the old lady. "I'm as sorry as you are that my great-granddaughter is dead, but what's done is done."

The King knew better than to argue with his grandmother. "What should I do, Grandmother?" he asked.

"Call your wise men together. Tell them you need to understand the WHEN and the WHAT and the WHO and the WHY."

"The WHEN and the WHAT and the WHO and the WHY?" repeated the King in astonishment. "But Grandmother, I don't understand."

"Of course you don't, that's the trouble," said the old lady. "Just do as I say, and while you're about it, you may as well tell the Queen to come and speak with me." So the Queen came next, walking down the long corridors, trailing her black robes and holding her handkerchief to her eyes.

"You're a pretty sight," snapped the old lady when she saw her.

"My heart is broken," sobbed the Queen.

"Fiddlesticks, it's because you're very sad. And in the meanwhile my meals don't come on time, and the corridors aren't cleaned, and no one attends to the garden. I won't have it."

"But Grandmother . . ." began the Queen.

"Don't grandmother me," interrupted the old lady. "I'm sad too, but it's time we all started living again."

Now the Queen was not as used to the grandmother's ways as her husband, and she tried to argue. "If you were a mother and your little daughter had died . . ." she began.

"I was a mother long before you were born—and what's more, I buried three children as well," said the grandmother. "Now this is what you must do. Call together all the servants and tell them you need to understand the WHEN and the WHAT and the WHO and the WHY."

"I don't understand," said the Queen in astonishment.

"Of course you don't, that's just the trouble." And the old lady rapped on the floor with her stick to show that the interview was over.

The King called his nine wise men together. They had all served his father, and one had served his grandfather as well. They gathered before the sad King in the throne room.

"I need to understand the WHEN and the WHAT and the WHO and the WHY," he told them. The wise men nodded solemnly and put their heads together. They said one thing and another until finally they came to an agreement. Then the one who had served his grandfather stood before the King.

"The WHEN has to do with time, your Majesty," he said. "Time is a mystery, for it has no beginning and no end, and on no account can it be stopped. WHEN is past, as well as present, as well as future—these are all one; they cannot be separated."

All the wise men nodded to show they agreed. "The WHAT, your Majesty, has to do with objects and with situations. The WHAT also has to do with space, which is another mystery, for space cannot be measured, nor can it be seen nor heard nor tasted nor touched nor smelled. Objects, on the other hand, can be seen and heard and tasted and touched and smelled, but only by those beings who have eyes and ears and tongues and hands and noses to do so. Yet since those objects can only exist in space, which *cannot* be seen or heard or tasted or touched or smelled, then there is a question whether the objects exist at all. And in any case, since situations can only exist if a moment is caught in time, and since we have already seen that time can on no account be stopped, then we must conclude that situations do not truly exist, which means that objects do not exist either, for objects cannot exist without a situation to contain them."

The oldest wise man stopped to catch his breath, looking pleased with himself. By this time the King was rather confused, but he furrowed his brow and tried to look as if he were following.

"The WHO, your Majesty, are those beings who can see and hear and taste and touch and smell. The WHO always exist within the WHEN, and in relationship to the WHAT, and since we have already seen that neither the WHEN nor the WHAT can truly be said to exist, then no doubt there is also some question as to whether the WHO exists either."

All the wise men were nodding and smiling, and even though the King was thoroughly confused by now, he furrowed his brow once more and nodded in return. Then the oldest wise man cleared his throat importantly.

"The WHY is too difficult for us, your Majesty. If the WHY could be understood, you would have no need of wise men."

Then the wise men bowed as low as they could manage, and in a dignified manner they filed out of the room. The King was left alone on his throne thinking about what they had said.

In the meanwhile the Queen had gathered all the servants into the upper chamber of the south tower, where she did her weaving. They all came crowding in, the cook and the footman and the coachman, the scullery maids and the serving maids, and the gardeners and stable boys. They found the sad Queen sitting beside her loom.

"I need to understand the WHEN and the WHAT and the WHO and the WHY," she told them.

The maids, gardeners, stable boys, the cook, footman, and the coachman all scratched their heads. Finally the cook spoke. She had been at the palace for twenty years and didn't mind speaking up to anyone.

"It's clear enough," she said. "The WHEN is the moment when the Princess fell into the millpond."

Everyone looked at her admiringly. Then the old footman stepped forward.

"The WHAT is that our own little Princess is dead," he quavered. They all looked at the floor and sighed.

The head gardener, who was a rough fellow and not very popular, spoke next.

"I say the WHO is that ninny of a nursemaid who stopped to talk to the stable boy when she ought to have been watching the Princess," he growled. Since both the nursemaid and the stable boy had been dismissed, nobody argued with him. They sighed again.

After a long silence, the youngest scullery maid spoke. "I don't know the WHY," she said timidly. "Perhaps there isn't any."

Everyone was very surprised that she had spoken at all. And they were even more surprised to find they couldn't disagree with her. They looked uncomfortable. They shifted their weight. They shuffled their feet. "Thank you," said the Queen. "That will do." So they made their bows and their curtsies and left the Queen alone.

After a time she stood up, and gathering her black robes about her, she hurried along the corridors, down the great stone stairway, until she found the King, still sitting on his throne and pondering what his wise men had told him.

"I have an idea," said the Queen. She was still holding her handkerchief, but it was not pressed to her eyes.

"That's more than I have," said the King gloomily.

"I think we should send messengers out across the Kingdom," said the Queen. "I think we should offer one hundred gold pieces to anyone who is able to tell us the WHY."

The King thought it a good idea, and in all the hustle and bustle that it took to send out the messengers, the palace began to stir again, and the servants began to attend to their duties. As the messengers went out far and wide, the country began to stir as well. People came out to listen to what the messengers had to say, meetings were held, and taverns opened up to hold the meetings. The taverns sent out word to the farmers, the fishermen, the butchers and bakers to bring in food for all the folk who were gathering—but since the fish were still not rising, the animals were still not giving birth, and the corn was still not growing, there was not much food to be had.

Now there was a particular farmer who was not satisfied with the way things were going. It was spring, and he had five children to feed.

He wanted to be out planting his corn, fishing his pond, and watching his animals being born.

"I'm sick and tired of it," he said one evening, as his family gathered around the supper table. It wasn't much of a supper, for there was no meat, nor fish, nor even any meal.

"It's a funny thing," he went on. "Here's the King wanting to know the WHY, the tavern wanting me to bring in food, the King's messenger wanting to give away one-hundred gold pieces, me wanting decent food on my table, and not one of us is getting what he wants."

"That's true," agreed his wife. "It's a funny thing."

"I say it's got to stop!" said the farmer.

"How will you stop it?" asked the wife.

"Well, we'd best start with what the King wants," said the farmer. (He'd been at the tavern during the day and had heard all the news.) "If the wise men can't tell the King what he wants to know, then it's not an answer that comes from being wise. If the folk in the palace can't tell him, then it's not an answer that comes from living in a palace. And since none of us in the tavern know, it's not an answer that comes from plain common sense. But still there're one-hundred gold pieces to be picked up, and I say we must find a way to have them."

His wife was busy serving the potatoes. She looked up, and she saw her children sitting around the table. "Perhaps the children can find out," she said. She was a good mother, and she was in the habit of listening to her children.

Her husband laughed at her and ate his potatoes. And that was all they said about it. But the children had been listening, and after supper they came together to talk about what they would do.

"I'll go to the pond tomorrow and see what I can find," said the oldest.

"I'll go into the field," said the second.

"I'll go to the orchard," said the third.

"I'll go into the woods," said the fourth.

"I'll stay in the kitchen garden and keep my eyes open," said the youngest.

The next morning the oldest boy, whose name was Conrad, went to the pond. The fish were not rising, but he saw a frog sitting on a lily pad. "Good morning," said Conrad. "Could you answer a question, please?"

"That depends," said the frog. "I'm not feeling at all well today."

"I'm sorry to hear that," said Conrad. "My question is, why do people have to die?"

"That's a foolish question," said the frog. "You'd much better ask why tadpoles have to lose their tails."

"But I don't want to know that," said Conrad. But, he was interested. "Maybe it's because things have to change if they're going to grow? Nothing *ever* stays the same."

"Well, maybe," said the frog. "But I didn't expect it would happen to me."

"Did you want to stay a tadpole all your life?" asked Conrad. "Then you couldn't sit on a lily pad and sun yourself."

"Hrmph," croaked the frog. A fly buzzed past, and the frog snatched it up.

"You see," laughed Conrad. "You couldn't catch flies either. But you haven't told me why people die."

"I don't have to," croaked the frog. "You already know," and it splashed into the pond.

The second boy, Henry, went wandering into the field. After a while he noticed something moving, and, when he looked, he saw it was a snake, straining and pushing.

"What are you doing?" Henry asked curiously.

"I'm getting rid of my skin," said the snake. "It's too tight."

Henry had never seen a snake shed its skin before, and he watched for a while. Presently, when the snake seemed to be resting, he said, "Do you mind if I ask you a question?"

"Go ahead," said the snake.

"Why do people die?" asked Henry.

The snake began wriggling again. "You mean, why do people shed their skins?" it said. "That's easy. It's because the old skin doesn't fit."

"It's not easy," said Henry. "The King doesn't know why, the folk in the palace don't know why, and my father doesn't know why."

The snake gave a final wriggle. "That just shows how stupid they are," it said. "There's my skin to prove it." And it slithered off into the tall grass.

The third boy, Jack, went into the orchard. There were young trees planted in rows, and plenty of half-grown ones, but he went straight to the biggest tree of all and stood looking up into its branches. It was a still day—not a leaf was stirring.

"Please," he called. "I need to understand why people die."

Then he waited. He was a patient boy, and he wasn't in a hurry. After a long while the branches began to stir. Perhaps a breeze had come up. Whatever it was, there was a sound that came with it, a rustling and a whispering, and the more he listened, the more he seemed to understand what the sound was saying.

"I suppose you think I never change," he heard.

Well, Jack hadn't been thinking anything at all, so he listened more.

"Come back in the summer, in the fall, in the winter. You'll see."

"See what?" asked Jack.

"The ebb and the flow of the seasons."

"That wasn't exactly what I wanted to know," said Jack.

"It is, though you don't know it. Look around you, Jack. What do you see?"

Jack looked around, and he saw the log of an old tree that had fallen the year before. Beside it he saw a young seedling, just coming into bud, thrusting its way up from the same root. He saw apple blossoms, flowers in bloom, and grass that was fresh and green.

"I see spring," he said.

The leaves rustled and whispered, but try as he would, Jack couldn't catch another word.

The fourth boy, Tom, went walking into the woods until he came to a hollow tree. He had found it a few days before, and he knew that a bear was living there. He peered inside, and sure enough, he saw something large and furry.

"Hello there," he shouted, "I need to know something." He was a brave boy and didn't mind waking up bears. The bear stirred, and after a bit its head appeared with one eye half open.

"You better be quick about it," said the bear. "There's a honeycomb here, and I'm not done with it."

"I don't see it," said Tom.

"Of course not, it's in my dream."

"I want to know why people die," said Tom.

The bear opened its other eye. "It depends on what you think is real," said the bear. "My honey is real when I'm asleep, but you can't see it because you're awake."

"What's that got to do with why people have to die?" asked Tom.

"Everything," said the bear. "It makes you ask different questions."

"I don't understand," said Tom.

"You will," said the bear. "It all depends on what you think is real." And it curled down into the tree.

The youngest was a girl named Maggie, and she went to play in the kitchen garden. She was keeping her eyes open. After a while she noticed a squirrel sitting on the garden wall. "Hello," said Maggie. "Do you happen to know why people die?"

The squirrel cocked its head and peered down at her. "I might," it said. "Are you sure that's what you want to know?"

"It's what *they* want to know," said Maggie. "I'd rather know Where than Why."

"Good," said the squirrel. "Let's play hide and seek." It scurried down the wall and into the vegetable rows. "Here I am," it called. "Peek-a-boo. Come and find me, Maggie."

They chased each other till Maggie was tired.

The squirrel laughed at her from behind a rock. "Just once more," it said. "It's your turn. Come and find me."

"But I can't, you're not here anymore." Maggie was peering behind the rock, quite exasperated. "Just when I think I've found you, you're already somewhere else."

"Good for you, Maggie, you guessed it." The squirrel was back on the wall again. "Don't you see?—That's what the game is all about. Don't forget now. I'm not gone—I'm only somewhere else!" And the squirrel scampered away.

At supper that evening the farmer was speaking about the hundred gold pieces again. "It's no good," he said to his wife. "All day long I sat in the tavern. I listened and I thought of this, and I listened some more and I thought of that, and the fact is, I'm no wiser than when I started."

The wife was lifting a pot from the stove. "That's a pity," she said. Then she turned to the children and looked at them with love in her eyes. "What were you doing all day?" she asked. "I hardly saw you."

"We were looking for the WHY," said Conrad.

"And what did you find?" asked the mother.

"I found that everything changes—otherwise nothing can grow," said Conrad.

"I found that you have to leave your old skin behind before you can wear a new one," said Henry.

"I found that there has to be summer and fall and winter before there can be spring," said Jack.

"I found that being asleep is real and being awake is real, but they're different," said Tom. "You can't be one when you're the other."

"I found that WHERE is more important than WHY," said Maggie. "Being dead is just being somewhere else."

The mother looked at her husband proudly. "You see?" she said.

The husband scratched his head in puzzlement. "I'm not sure it's just what the messenger wants," he said.

"Maybe not, but it will do the King good to hear it," said the wife. "You must go to the palace and tell him."

So the next morning the farmer put on his best clothes and climbed on his pony and set off for the palace. It was a day's journey, so he had time to turn things over in his mind. He came there at last and pulled the bell rope that hung at the great entrance. Presently the old footman opened the door.

"I've come about the WHY," said the farmer.

"Well, that's good," said the footman, and he brought the farmer to the throne room, where the King and the Queen were sitting on their thrones looking sad as ever.

The farmer bowed, though he wasn't used to bowing to anyone. "Your Majesties, I've come about the WHY," he said.

The King brightened, and the Queen took her handkerchief from her eyes. "Go on," said the King.

"Well, it's like this, your Majesty. If there's to be growing, there's got to be change. It's not natural for things to stay the same. And it's like this. In nature, what's old has to go before what's new can take its place. And it's like this—there's a time for budding and blossoming, and a time for leafing and fruiting, and a time for harvest, and a time for rest. And without the resting, there'll be no harvest next year."

The King nodded thoughtfully. "That's true," he said. "Every word of it."

"And it's like this," said the farmer. "Being alive is real and being dead is real, but they're not the same. You can't be one when you're the other. It's not sensible to ask when you're alive, why you're not dead, and it's not sensible to ask when you're dead, why you're not alive."

The King nodded again. "I think that's true too," he said. "I think it's probably what my wise men were trying to tell me."

He turned to the Queen. "What do you think, my dear?"

The Queen was looking at her hands, folded in her lap. "It may be what you need," she said, "And it may satisfy your grandmother, but to tell the truth, it doesn't help me at all."

The farmer cleared his throat awkwardly. "There's just one more thing," he said. "When all's said and done, it's WHERE that makes the difference. When you're dead, you're not gone. You're somewhere else."

The Queen sighed a long sigh. Then she looked up. "Yes," she said. "I believe you're right. After all, it's WHERE that makes the difference."

So the farmer got his hundred gold pieces, the grandmother got her meals served properly, and the King and Queen began to rule again. And the farmer hadn't been home long before he saw that the fish were starting to rise in his pond and the animals were ready to give birth in his barn, and soon after he planted his field, he saw that all up and down the long rows, the corn was starting to grow.

PAMELA MAYER is a Jungian adult-education specialist, an eighty-year-old grandmother, and a lover of woods, gardens, and fairy tales. Exploring the spiritual dimensions of life-threatening illness and death itself has led her to write "When the Princess Died," as well as a puppet show for children, *What Does Dead Mean?*

ETHAN GILSDORF

Sick Infant, Recovered

for Gabriel Turab O'Brien

Something dropped from the sky,
staining your skin, crossing your wires,
causing a small fire in your heart.
You thought of lacing your boots
for the return journey
up the soft tunnel of your mother.
No one would have blamed you, Gabriel,
lost for a time, a button, a broken compass
stuck on south, a hair snip softly falling
like a comet to the floor.

> The clouds issue a small apology:
> *We should have fixed this kid*
> *before sending him through the dolphin slot,*
> *the sliver between water and sky,*
> *to the cumulonimbus of his crib.*

Luckily, more than luck, the button
was discovered in everyone's desk drawers.
The button knew where it belonged,
and summoned its needle and thread,
the maker and fixer, to bind your four holes
firmly to the backdrop of tattered fabric.

[Artist unknown].
Baby in Red Chair.
Oil on canvas,
ca. 1810–1830.
Abby Aldrich Rockefeller
Folk Art Museum,
Williamsburg, Virginia.

Your compass found its pole.
And from your head, Gabriel, every day
blooms a thousand wildflowers.
Welcome. Welcome again.

ETHAN GILSDORF's poems have appeared in *Massachusetts Review, Southern Poetry Review, Connecticut Review, Hawai'i Review, Crazyhorse, The Christian Science Monitor, Exquisite Corpse,* and *Yankee*. His essays, reviews, and fiction have been published in *Poets & Writers, American Bookseller, The Quarterly,* and *New York Quarterly*. The former poetry editor of the *New Delta Review*, Gilsdorf won the Hobblestock Peace Poetry Competition (sponsored by the *Monserrat Review*) and was named a semifinalist for the "Discovery"/*The Nation* contest and three first-poetry book prizes.

WESLEY McNAIR

My Finite Eyes

Joan Miró.
Self-Portrait, I.
Pencil, crayon,
and oil on canvas,
57½×38¼ inches,
1937–1938.
The Museum of Modern
Art, New York. James
Thrall Soby Bequest.
Photograph ©2000
The Museum of Modern
Art, New York.
Artists Rights Society,
New York.

WHAT THEY SEE—the nurse watching the operation and the surgeon making his incision in the center of my left eye—I try to picture; the eye clamped open and staring up from its hole in the blue drape placed on my face. Grotesque as it is, the image doesn't bother me. I am peacefully sedated, and I gaze with my other eye into a cloudy blue that is the exact color of my contentment. Far off to the left, as if I were dreaming it, I am aware of a puddle, shaking in blue light. This is all I know of what the surgeon is doing, though I detect, in the long pauses of his conversation, his absorption.

"I've got something in my eye," we sometimes say, though the thing we have is more on the eye than in it. A cataract, on the other hand, is in it—the lens become an opaque pebble that makes lights splay and words disappear. My cataract is what the doctor has taken out. And now, the next day, he reaches for my eye patch to see how he has done. I think of the scene from the old movie; Bogart as an escaped convict, watching the doctor peel the bandages from his facial surgery. Only the doctor knows what the convict looks like now in his new identity, yet you can tell from the doctor's smile he is pleased. I examine the face of my own surgeon, but he just frowns, swinging a chin-rest, then a light toward me. There is silence as I position my chin and stare into more blue, a furry circle of it this time, and he explores with his painful point of white light. At last, I hear his word for what he has discovered; beautiful. Like Bogart himself, I am now a free man.

On the way home in a dry snowfall, my son driving, I recall Emerson, who wrote in his essay "Nature" that while he was in the woods, nothing could befall him—"no disgrace, no calamity (leaving me my eyes) which nature cannot repair." Leaving me my eyes! Enclosing the phrase in parentheses, Emerson snatched his eyes right out of that famous covenant with nature as if to say, These, I don't make deals with. Pleased by my doctor's report and glad to live in a century when surgeons can repair the things that nature cannot, I am drawn to winter on the road as I have never quite seen it. There is a thin dust of snow across the tail-lights of the car ahead that gives them a soft, bright glow. Past the town sign, gusts of snow swirl, tangle, and edge away from a hundred white cracks in the pavement as we pass. But more compelling still are the snowy woods that come toward us, opening to let the road through, then wider to let us through, the high branches of pines sheltering us for a quarter mile.

"You are too young for cataracts!" a friend exclaims when I tell him about the success of my operation. In fact, I am exactly the right age. My father got them in his fifties, inheriting from his elders the early cataract gene which he then passed on to me. The day after surgery, I think of what it must have been like for my father, who left the family in my childhood, when both of his lenses went dark. Victimized by high blood pressure and an ailing heart, he was considered a poor risk for anesthesia, so his cataracts were never removed. In his last months his vision got so bad, according to a relative, he labored in the backyard garden lying on his side. That close to his work, he could just make out the difference between the seed plants and the weeds. What his thoughts were as he weeded, having left some of his own seed behind to grow as it would without his help, the relative didn't say—only that he lived in a dimness, unable to read or to bear bright lights, until the day he died. At the very age of my father as he lay in that garden, I feel the more keenly the sadness of his life and recall, too, all the trouble he passed on to me apart from my cataracts. I am relieved I have at least been able to rid myself of this trouble.

Unfortunately, however, my relief does not last. Concerned about my double vision a week after the operation, I consult a new surgeon, filling in while my own is on vacation. The new doctor, who has nothing to do with gentleness or care, shakes drops in my eye and reaches for her tools. Then in she goes, pressing a contact lens against my eye with the narrow end of a metal cone. Holding the cone fast, she shines a light inside it that is so bright, I shut my other eye and pop the contact lens out. "I'm sorry," I tell her, hoping—I am so compliant, so willing to have her savage me this way—she'll see the error of her aggressiveness. But she is now impatient with me and even more aggressive. When the session is finished, I am wandering in the parking lot, blind in one eye and unable to find my car. Going up and down the rows, I hear her voice in my head—its certainty that I've done something wrong. "You must be more careful in the future," it says. "That implant has become decentered."

"At fifty we're so fragile," Robert Lowell—that chronicler of eye problems—wrote about his increasing nearsightedness in "Myopia: a Night." Waiting the next four days for my vacationing surgeon to return, I feel the middle-age fragility Lowell referred to. And I remember the bad eye-trouble Lowell described in another poem, "Eye and Tooth"—his cut cornea, which caused a turmoil of pain, memory, and self-recrimination. I begin to suffer my own self-recrimination, convincing myself in the end that the substitute doctor is right; the decentered implant is my fault. I've bent over too far or lifted something heavy without thinking and caused the nearly invisible hooks at the left and right of the implant to slip. Yet when my surgeon sees me again, he does not accuse me. The decentering could have been caused by any number of things, he says, even by a small vacuum that may have settled, unbeknownst, under the implant. He draws a Mickey Mouse eye with a slipped implant to show me how my eye looks; meanwhile, I watch the double image of his thumb and fingers moving on the tablet, wondering if his hand itself could be the culprit. No, I decide; too many others have praised this surgeon's work. The relative stillness of that drawing hand, which barely moved moments ago when I shook it, shows how steady it would be under pressure.

At this writing, I await the new surgery. My surgeon's hand will make a wider incision for a new implant, this one so big, no slipping later on will matter. The day after, I will return for a third rerun of myself as Bogart watching my surgeon remove the bandage. For I have already been in his office twice now with a patch, the first time two years ago, after cataract surgery on my right eye.

What happened in the weeks following that operation I'm hoping now to avoid; the tearing of the retina, and a great dread of retinal detachment. The only way of mending the tears, it turned out, was to apply laser beams carefully calibrated in intensity. By my side to apply them in his dark room was the doctor, wearing an odd, cone-shaped hat made of metal. "Six hundred," he said to his assistant, and pressed a pedal, sending white light into my eye from the point of his hat. "Seven hundred," he said. "Nine hundred." Each time, I felt a dull pain and simultaneously beheld a large, beautiful planet that contained several tiny, red rivers. Listening to the numbers and watching that mysterious orb in the dark, I could have been among the priests of an occult religion, learning by some strange ritual the secrets of the universe. Then I realized what I saw was no planet; it was a reflection of my eye.

Yet to see the eye as so vast a thing is not to misrepresent it. For losing our eyes, we would lose nothing less than the whole world. We would be like the speaker in Emily Dickinson's poem 327, who "got [her] eye put out," and now yearns for all she once had:

> But were it told to me—Today—
> That I might have the sky
> For mine—I tell you that my Heart
> Would split, for size of me—
>
> The meadows—mine—
> The Mountains—mine—
> All Forests—Stintless Stars—
> As much of Noon as I could take
> Between my finite eyes—
>
> The Motions of the Dipping Birds—
> The Morning's Amber Road—
> For mine—to look at when I liked—
> The News would strike me dead—

Months after she played the sightless narrator of this poem, Dickinson suffered an eye disorder that actually took away her sight, suddenly experiencing the "death" she had earlier imagined, without forests or mountains, dipping birds or amber road. By what marvel of perception this poet was able to look ahead to her own malady and prepare herself for the treatments that finally restored her vision, it would be hard to say. I only know that now, as I reread Dickinson's poem, it helps to prepare me for the treatments I myself will now undergo, however demanding they may be. For having known the world of the eye—its various geography and incomparable beauty—who would willingly give up any part of it?

WESLEY MCNAIR is the recipient of Rockefeller, Guggenheim, National Education Association, and Fulbright fellowships. He has been awarded prizes from *Poetry, Poetry Northwest,* and *Yankee* magazines. This fall, David Godine will publish a book of McNair's personal and critical essays, *Mapping the Heart: Reflections on Place and Poetry,* which will include "My Finite Eyes." A new book of his poems, *Fire,* is forthcoming from Godine in 2001. His other volumes of verse are *The Faces of Americans in 1853, The Town of No, My Brother Running, Talking in the Dark,* and a chapbook, *Twelve Journeys in Maine.* He directs the bachelor of fine arts program in creative writing at the University of Maine at Farmington.

STEVEN LAUTERMILCH

For an Ancient Artist

Clear Creek Canyon,
Sevier County, Utah

A millennium one to two ago
he leaned for an hour or another
over this newspaper rock
and worked until his work and prayer

were one. He had no name
or, if he did, none of the language
we give his age, his culture,
his humanity, his art.

Now a concrete path
paves the way where he once climbed
and sat, a shadow on sandstone that sought
only vision, left only these marks.

What is it a sheep means
to say except its unspoken name,
his or hers, mine
and yours.

Let these lines
hold still as many days
and hours. As his.
As ours.

Opposite:
Nine-Mile Canyon.
Duchesne County, Utah.
Photographed
by Steve Lautermilch.

A poet and photographer, STEVEN LAUTERMILCH lives on the Outer Banks of North Carolina, where he offers workshops in dream study, meditation, and writing. This past fall he spent in the Southwest, camping and hiking, photographing the prehistoric rock art of the native Americans. His chapbook of poems, *Triangle, Circle, Square,* won the 1998 *Ruah* competition.

JOHN HITCHCOCK

The Call of Stone

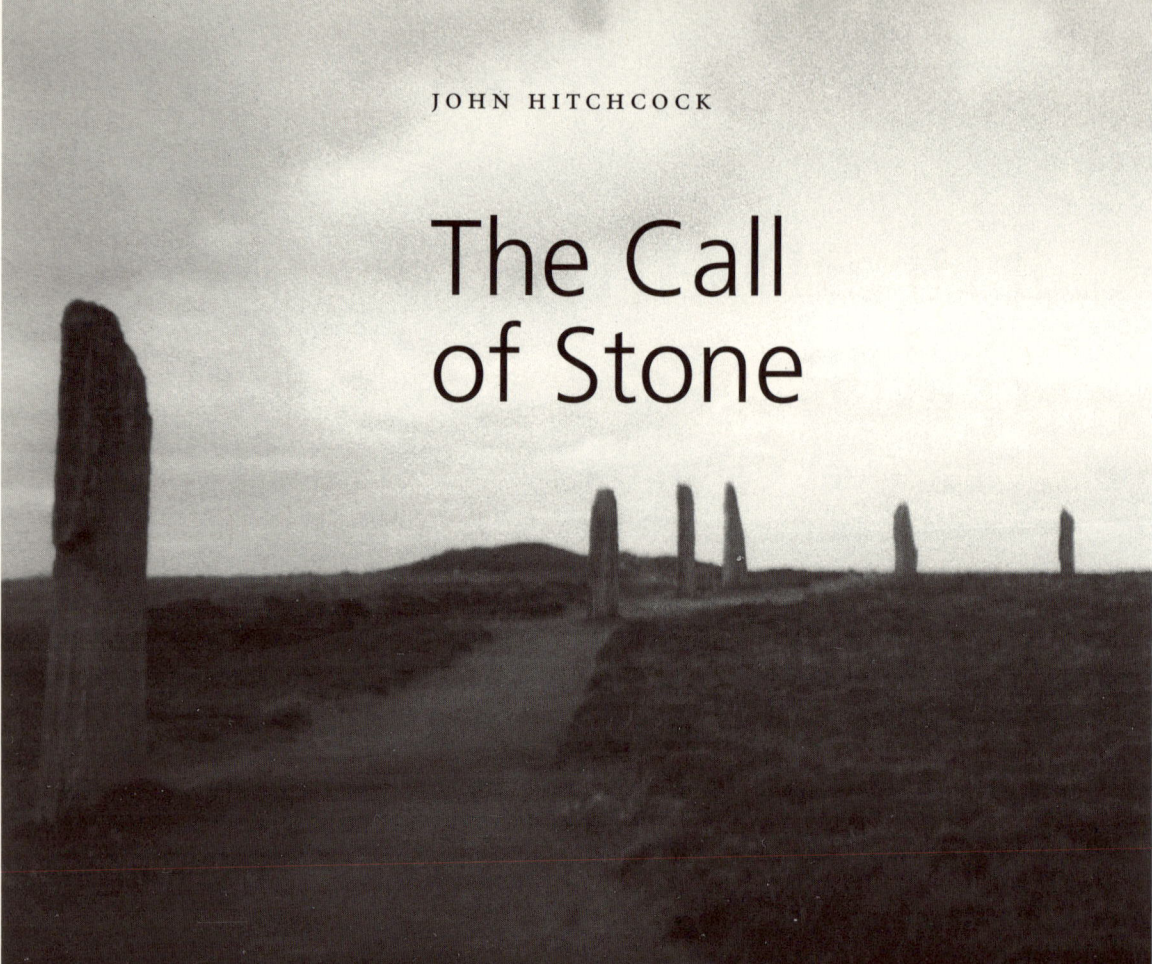

Alice B. Skinner.
Ring of Brogar,
Orkney Islands, Scotland.
Photograph, June 2000.

The stone of a world lies helpless 'til I come.
The oil of a world may light no lamp,
may heal no wound until I come.
Lost with stars, sky fills itself with breath to
blow out torches of a world unless I come.
An entire pregnant universe waits upon me...
—SHEILA MOON, SONGS FOR WANDERERS

WHAT IS STONE that, if a Moses strikes it, it becomes a living spring? What is stone that, when we hold it, we feel the power and steadiness of the Earth moving within ourselves and can draw upon it for our own steadiness and power? What is stone that it can ask us to raise it from the ground to become a sanctuary of the divine?

Stone asks something of us. We ponder it both in body and in mind; it is not something wholly outside ourselves. We feel it as most solid, but we don't just walk on it; we raise it up so that we may walk among stones as among gods. That which is most solid also seems to embody some of the greatest power of spirit. It is spirit-matter; it is the Earth reaching upward from within itself. And, as the epigram suggests, the stone is waiting for us and wanting us to raise it so. J.R.R. Tolkien wrote of this intuition of the feeling stones in *The Fellowship of the Ring*. The protagonists of the story are walking in a land that has been empty for centuries. One of them speaks:

> There is a wholesome air about Hollin. Much evil must befall a country before it wholly forgets the elves, if once they dwelt there.
>
> That is true, said Legolas, but the elves of this land were a race strange to us of the sylvan folk, and the trees and the grass do not now remember them. Only I hear the stones lament them: Deep they delved us; fair they wrought us; high they built us, but now they are *gone*. (p.339; Ballantine, 1955, 1965, 1982.)

For over thirty years I have been associated with a seminar center in northern California, a 300-acre ritual space. In 1975, we wanted to do something special for the centennial of the birth of C.G. Jung, and, in roaming the woods and streams on the property, I discovered a beautiful stone of about 700 pounds weight that we decided to bring to the center of our ritual meadow. We scheduled it into the next men's work weekend.

Alice B. Skinner.
Ring of Brogar,
Orkney Islands, Scotland.
Photograph, June 2000.

The usual atmosphere of work at those weekends is that there are a lot of opinions as to how to do various jobs, and there were, on this occasion, several men present who were particularly prone to "take over" the directing of jobs. Our task was to lift the stone from the creek to a Landrover on the bank, which we proposed to do by rolling the stone onto a piece of plywood large enough for us all to get around and lift onto the bank and into the vehicle.

It was really an awkward job, but we did it with seeming ease. Reflecting afterwards, we realized that there had been absolute co-operation with no tendency for anyone to take over. We all felt that the stone itself had directed our actions. It was as if the stone wanted to become part of our rituals.

AT ABOUT THE TIME THAT THE FIRST CIVILIZATIONS AROSE in the Middle East, prior to the pyramid-building period in Egypt, a culture flourished in the west of Europe that raised great stones. For that reason we have called it the Megalithic culture. The stones are virtually all that we have with which to understand or feel what might have been moving in those people, yet they suffice to tell us much, for the labor that went into this work is almost incomprehensible. From that fact alone, we can intuit a tremendous calling of the spirit. In the patterns of the stones, also, we know that this calling was related to the heavens, for the movements of the Sun, the Moon, and many stars are documented in detail.

When the pyramids arose in Egypt, it was by the will of the Pharaohs using the labor of slaves. Julian Jaynes in *The Origin of Consciousness in the Breakdown of the Bicameral Mind* has pointed out that such works were done in response to what was felt, even heard, as the *command* of a god or a deeply spiritual call. In a much later time, the same call came to those who raised up the great cathedrals of the Gothic era, but now with the free devotion of the people of the communities involved. It is difficult from the perspective of our own times to realize, even to imagine, that the stones of these enormous churches were hand-carried or winched to the height of hundreds of feet. When we ponder that fact, however, we gain a greater grasp of the devotion and energy of a whole culture lavished upon these buildings that typically took a century to complete.

An account of an individual experience gives an insight which I think can be extrapolated to whole cultures, for it is a cultural expression in itself. It is a part of the story of Jacob, found at Genesis 27:11–22 (Revsided Standard Version):

> And [Jacob] came to a certain place, and stayed there that night, because the sun had set. Taking one of the stones of the place, he

put it under his head and lay down in that place to sleep. And he dreamed that there was a ladder set up on the earth, and the top of it reached to heaven; and behold, the angels of God were ascending and descending on it. And the *Lord* stood above it and said, "I am the *Lord,* the God of Abraham your father, and the God of Isaac; the land on which you lie I will give to you and to your descendants; and your descendants shall be like the dust of the earth, and you shall spread abroad to the west and to the east and to the north and to the south; and by you and your descendants shall all the families of the earth bless themselves. Behold I am with you and will keep you wherever you go, and I will not leave you until I have done that of which I have spoken to you."

Then Jacob awoke from his sleep and said, "Surely the *Lord* is in this place, and I did not know it." And he was afraid, and said, "How awesome is this place. This is none other than the house of God, and this is the gate of heaven."

So Jacob rose early in the morning and he took the stone which he had put under his head and he set it up for a pillar and poured oil on the top of it.

He called the name of that place Bethel . . . Then Jacob made a vow, saying, "If God will be with me, and will keep me in this way that I go, and will give me bread to eat and clothing to wear, so that I come again to my father's house in peace, then the *Lord* shall be my God, and this stone which I have set up for a pillar, shall be God's house . . .

Here the stone is the implied source of the dream of God, and it is set up as a pillar and anointed with oil as a king, prophet, or messiah might be. It is even destined to be named the house of God. But what moved Jacob to lift it to a standing position is not told in the story. Whatever it was, it speaks across ages to the feeling I am trying to describe. And whatever it was, it may as well be ascribed to the stone calling to Jacob from within to perform this ritual act.

At one time there were over 900 stone circles in the British Isles, of which the massive site at Avebury near Stonehenge with a whole modern village at its center was the largest. In Brittany, the same Megalithic culture raised a 350-ton stone whose top soared 66 feet above the ground. This is Er Grah, the "stone of the fairies," which had been shaped like a great long tear drop. It now lies shattered into four pieces since it fell, most likely some time in the twelfth century. For comparison, the largest obelisk erected by the Egyptians weighed less than 250 tons. Er Grah was the center of the largest lunar observatory of the prehistoric world, with sighting lines for the rising of the Moon up to ten miles in length.

Near this ancient observatory were erected stone rows containing in all over 3000 stones, hundreds of which weigh ten or more tons each. Tens or hundreds of thousands of people might have stood among them to honor the sunrise of the summer solstice, toward which the rows of stones are generally oriented.

Of the stone circles of Britain, the largest ones are the oldest. Those with diameters of 100 meters or more date generally from around 3000 BCE, and include Stonehenge, Long Meg and her Daughters in the Lake District, and the Ring of Brodgar on the Isle of Orkney. It is thought that such large enclosures were meant for the participation of the whole community, and that the smaller ones erected later were used more by a priestly group on behalf of the populace. It may also be that the feeling for massive raising of stones had peaked after the dozen or so centuries of the flourishing of the culture, and that works raising stones on such an intensive scale would have to wait for a new surge of the religious spirit, as indeed happened in other times and places.

These Megalithic stones were not merely found and erected. The stones of the main circle and the trilithons at Stonehenge, weighing 30 to 50 tons, were not only brought 20 miles to the site; they were literally carved out of a huge mass of solid rock and shaped or "dressed" by pounding with other stones until they met the architectural needs as to size, as well as an aesthetic need. Other stones at Stonehenge, the 5-ton "bluestones," were brought hundreds of miles from western Wales to be part of this temple.

CULTURES BUILD MONUMENTS OF STONE, and by the beauty of these works we value the spirit of the culture that made them. The Egyptians made statues of gods, goddesses, queens, and kings of the hardest, most refractory stone available, and carved a deep spirituality into their forms and faces. The colossal winged figures carved in granite by the Assyrians, guardians of the palace ten and twelve feet high (now in the British Museum), strike awe into the soul of us "moderns" even if we imagine them being carved with power tools, as our own monumental sculptures are. They were not; they were shaped and polished by hand.

Of such statues, Jaynes asserts that the texts and other artworks of the times clearly indicate that those who made them heard them speak with real voices, voices of gods quite literally, and that these voices really did guide those communities, even creating and shaping their civilizations. The ability to hear these voices subsided as societies grew more complex and as what we know as individual consciousness grew stronger and more prevalent.

There is something about the awakening of human consciousness and the rising of stone—something that senses a solid foundation beneath and begins to stand up, to reach upward. Stone is not something wholly outside ourselves; it evokes our awareness of an inner ground of *being*. It seems that the *work* of wrestling with stone to raise it is somehow essential to the building of a solid center in human beings.

In 1980, I led a small group to visit a stone circle in a tiny community. At that time, we were welcomed by the local farmers, who swung open the gates and invited us to drive to the circle. Later, when the site became well known and was visited by many tourists, the locals permitted thorn bushes to overgrow the site to protect it. The last tour of standing stones that I led was in 1995. At that time we were privileged to have an hour by ourselves in Stonehenge after it closed for the day. Wandering individually among these tall figures, we listened for their voices. They are now silent as to words, but their spiritual power is still present and potent. When will stones call us once more to lift them into a new spiritual form for the deepening of our consciousness?

JOHN HITCHCOCK holds graduate degrees in clinical mental-health counseling, phenomenology of science and religion, and astronomy. He has taught mythology and astronomy at San Francisco State University and physics at the University of Wisconsin at La Crosse. For over thirty years he has led seminars with the Guild for Psychological Studies in San Francisco, specializing in mythology and in science as a source of numinous symbols for personal growth and daily living. Dr. Hitchcock is the author of four books in science and spirituality, including *Healing Our Worldview: The Unity of Science and Religion,* Swedenbog Foundation, 1999), and *The Heart's Home: A Vision of the Universe,* which will be published by the Swedenborg Foundation in 2000. John and his wife Carrie have recently moved to Maine where he works as a clinical mental-health counselor.

Mike Taylor. Pen-and-ink, 1999.

"LET'S JUST SAY HE INVENTED THE WHEEL AND LEAVE IT AT THAT."

ROSALIND BAKER WILSON

Pittsburgh— Revisited

Charles C. Hofmann. *View of Henry Z. Van Reed's Farm, Papermill, and Surroundings.* Oil on canvas, 1872. Abby Aldrich Rockefeller Folk Art Museum, Williamsburg, Virginia.

MY MOTHER WAS MARY BLAIR, known as The O'Neill Actress. She came from Pittsburgh, and her family was Swedenborgian. Her second husband was my father, Edmund Wilson, journalist and critic, whom she had been initially drawn to as he bore the same name as her oldest brother Edmund. She was my father's first wife. I was born when she was twenty-nine. She died at the age of fifty-two on my birthday, September 19, 1946, after a long struggle with tuberculosis.

She was a favorite actress of both O'Neill and the renowned journalist and theater critic, Brooks Atkinson. She had been in the first graduating class of the Carnegie Institute's drama department and was one of the three original women members of the Theater Guild.

Her health had chronically failed as a result of a severe case of whooping cough and the public persecution she endured because she knelt on stage and kissed Paul Robeson's hand in the initial production of O'Neill's *All God's Chillun Got Wings*. That scene resulted in widespread attacks by the Ku Klux Klan, the Anti-Vice League, and Women's Clubs all over the country. This was before Eleanor Roosevelt broke with the Daughters of the American Revolution over Marian Andersen singing at the Lincoln Memorial. My mother, O'Neill, and the cast caused a widespread racist fuss. The opposing forces threatened to kidnap the children of the actors, to bomb the theater and the cast.

At forty, she was told by her doctors that she had tuberculosis and must be hospitalized. She had to back out of co-starring in a role she had just accepted. When her doctor asked her where she wished to go, she said to her hometown, Pittsburgh, although she didn't suppose it was a great place for her ailment. He said it had one of the best hospitals in the country, the Tuberculosis Institute.

From then on, I went out once a year to visit her and stay with her good-sized Swedenborgian family. I was eleven when she was taken to Pittsburgh and twenty-three when she died.

Before that I had been taken west occasionally by my mother to visit her own mother, my maternal grandmother Blair, who had come from Quincy, Massachusetts. Her father was the Reverend William A. Fuller, an Episcopalian minister. He became a "New-Church" convert through the writings of Emanuel Swedenborg and openly preached Swedenborgian tenets as pastor of the Episcopalian church in Montrose, Pennsylvania. As a result, he was compelled to resign and died two years later.

My grandfather Blair's family came from Coleraine, Northern Ireland, where they were flax growers and linen makers. They had graduated from thatched to frame domiciles. He had come to Pittsburgh in 1880 at the age of nineteen with a teaching certificate and eventually became for ten years city editor of the *Pittsburgh Post* and for a while owned a paper, *The Alleghenian*. My grandmother Blair lived in a large comfortable old house at Walnut and Ivy Streets in Pittsburgh. A true corner house, you could see the goings-on down Ivy from one set of windows and the neighborhood bustle on Walnut from another side. There was a large encircling front porch—a drugstore on the opposite corner and a few blocks away an overhead railroad bridge spanning eight or so tracks from which you could see the trains coming and going east and west.

Grandmother Blair had six children, Edmund, the oldest, born on May 29, the day before the Johnstown Flood. By May 30, there were three feet of water in the living room. Edmund's siblings were

Lois, Mary, Bill, and Venita. Lois and my mother were to have rather stormy emotional lives with several marriages before settling down, whereas Venita became a trained nurse and had a serene marriage with six children. My father attributed this to the fact that things were more settled in the family when she came along. Others may have felt her involvement with the New Church (as the Swedenborgian church organization was called) was responsible.

My grandmother Blair was much interested in the arts and had a beautiful singing voice. She was in touch with all the visiting artists, and a large grand piano dominated the living room. She kept up a lively correspondence with the novelist Henry James' father who was a devoted Swedenborg reader and lecturer.

After the onset of my mother's illness and the death of Grandmother Blair, I usually stayed with Uncle Ed and his family. He had married the daughter of a Swedenborgian minister, Homer Synnesvedt, and had four children: Virginia, whom I adored and who was my own age, Jim, and two younger boys, Kenneth and Robert. They lived on a hill on Greymore Road.

Ed's wife, Lucille, was an energetic, handsome woman who made me feel part of her family. My uncle had spent his life in the printing business and in the Blair printing company while it existed. He had been taken out of school by his father to be office boy and had educated himself by going to the Carnegie library in the evenings. He followed the political cartoonists in the magazines, and his head was filled with the pithy slogans coined in his day, such as "Vote for McKinley" and "Fill the Dinner Pail."

Despite the sad visits to my mother, I relished my stays with the Blairs on Greymore Road. I climbed the hill to the hospital to see the failing person whose physical being seemed to barely exist after a drastic operation that removed some of her ribs and left her hunchbacked. Ninety pounds was her weight at its best. She and my Aunt Lois had not so much left the Swedenborgian Church as wandered away from it. But my mother saw visions, and certainly some element of the spiritual plane kept her alive.

The warmth and positive atmosphere of the Edmund Blair household were contagious. Lucille Blair's father, the minister Homer Synnesvedt, a delightful and loveable man, was often around. There were happy references to his camp, which sounded like Shangri-la, and constant talk of that Swedenborgian stronghold, Bryn Athyn. It was a relief from the isolationism of my grandmother Wilson's household in New Jersey where I had been taken permanently when threats to kidnap the children of the actors were aired during the *All God's Children* donnybrook.

On several occasions, my father came out west with me. My cousin Kenneth Blair reminds me that my father had once taken a taxi from Philadelphia to Greymore Road, which impressed Kenneth no end. But the fact is my father had no car, and on Cape Cod we went everywhere on our bicycles. On one visit Ed was doing an article on labor relations, and we visited the Heinz plant with its happy workers sending catsup out into the world as opposed to the unhappy situation in the steel mills.

The arrival on the Pullman sleeper from New York to Pittsburgh was exciting; as we reached that town, the vitality of the West seemed to seep into the train itself. Even at the early morning arrival, I felt happily expectant, the great blast furnaces like dragons, the romantic names of the three rivers, the Ohio, the Allegheny, the Monongahela, and the anticipation of the fuss my Pittsburgh relatives would make over me. They didn't know my everyday faults, and I looked forward to the happy camaraderie engendered by my Swedenborgian relatives. My cousin Virginia had Titian hair and a happy manner, both fun-loving and courageous.

One summer when faux sharkskin was in as a dress material as well as Tyrolean suspenders from Lanz of Salzburg, I brought her a pair from New York like mine. She already had the ersatz sharkskin. We set off for downtown Pittsburgh in our two-piece outfits to shop and go to Huyler's restaurant. Reeking of Elizabeth Arden's latest perfume, *Blue Grass,* which my mother had given me, we were also singing, "She promised she would meet me when the clock struck seventeen at the stockyards a mile out of town," and the latest romantic song of the moment, "I let a song go out of my heart, the sweetest song I knew." Some University of Pittsburgh students asked us to lunch but we demurred, all song and make-believe sharkskin, but cowards at heart. Still we had been noticed in our hot attire, hoisted by our loudly embroidered suspenders. We had dared.

My mother's older sister, Lois, had started the Lois Blair Stock Company and had remained involved in the theater and the arts. She had happily married a newspaper man who had come to interview her—Roy Jansen, who for years wrote a column for the American Medical Association. Some of these columns dealt with folk remedies that worked. The Jansens had no children and made me feel gifted and competent, an attitude very different from my father's critical approach to life. Lois at her ending was to spend long hours with the Swedenborgian minister, shooing everyone else away.

My Aunt Venita lived with her husband Gilbert Smith in my grandmother Blair's old house at Walnut and Ivy. Gilbert was connected through his mother to a prominent Swedenborgian family, the Pitcairns, of Pittsburgh Plate Glass. Venita and Gilbert's lives centered about the New Church. He would eventually become head of the home economics department of Pittsburgh Gas.

After my mother's funeral I lost touch with my Pennsylvania relatives except for Christmas communications with the Jansens. I later found out this was partly through the machinations of my stepmother. But after my father's death in 1972, I contacted them and went out west to see them.

When I got off the plane, Gilbert Smith met me and took me to the top of a hill to look down on the new Pittsburgh. All the old excitement returned as I saw the lights and remembered the great furnaces burning across the hills, the names of the three rivers so magical to me, Allegheny, Monongahela, creating the Ohio.

The Smiths gave a party. Aunt Alicia had married my Uncle Bill, who had been in the Blair printing business, a natty bachelor at the time. She had been a pretty, fragile woman, with an attractive somewhat flighty manner, but had proved to be a rock of Gibraltar when the chips were down. The renegade, Lois, talked happily of "The doll of a church nearby." I learned that Virginia had married a Swedenborgian minister, Kenneth Stroh, who had served in Detroit and abroad, in London. She died in 1971. I felt an aching sadness when I heard of her death and remembered the day we had thought we were the bees knees and sashayed into Huyler's in all our finery.

In 1974 Gilbert and Venita drove Lois up from Sarver, Pennsylvania, where she was in a nursing home manned by my cousin Kenneth Blair, to my home in northern New York: Talcottville in Lewis County known as the North Country in the foothills of the Adirondacks. Venita and Gilbert were full of energy after the long drive. They meditated in the afternoon, and I noted that they seemed full of their faith, more aglow than either Lois or myself although we had a jolly time by all. I can still see Gilbert sitting in the Boston rocker in my living room, talking of the spirits around us, looking out toward the Adirondacks, saying, "There must be Pitcairns there."

I loved their visit and regretted the years I had lost touch. I miss contact with the ones who have died. But then according to them, they're always around.

ROSALIND BAKER WILSON, WAS an editor at the Houghton Mifflin Co. from 1949 to 1958 and in 1963 and 1964. Her stories and memoirs have been published in the *Ladies Home Journal*, *The Saturday Evening Post*, *Gourmet*, and *Provincetown Arts*. She is author of *Memoir of the Masicich* (Grove).

PART II

Generational Constellations

ELIZABETH OAKES

The Woman Who Uttered Paradise

(after "The Sixth Day of Creation,"
a watercolor by Thomas Trevelyn, 1608)

Someone without much skill
painted this Eden, with its diluted
trees and grass, its fish and ocean
paled to amber. Only streaks
of blue for a sky. Birds curl,
seem to fall. No air yet.

Adam lies asleep. Eve rises
out of his side into the sun.
It's amber too, like the water.
No angels with gold leaf wings.
Even the sun is not in the sky.
It is in the green, around Eve.

Eve reaches into that sun,
toward a word. It is so right,
that beginning world, her rising,
a word in the sun. It is so right.

She is reaching for it now.

ELIZABETH OAKES is a tenured associate professor at Western Kentucky University where she teaches courses in American women poets and in Shakespeare. Her doctorate was granted by Vanderbilt University in 1991. She has published both scholarly works and her own poetry, with her most recent acceptances being by *Women's Studies: An Interdisciplinary Journal* and *The Southern Anthology*.

MARSHA DUBROW

That's All Right Mama

ELVIS PRESLEY, the quintessential symbol of the generation gap, actually united Mother and me. This is no Elvis sighting story; it's an Elvis listening story.

Mother was among the first Houstonians to hear Elvis on the radio. Her favorite music, aside from opera and Dixieland, was gospel—long before gospel, much less country, was cool among Caucasians.

Richard Lindner.
Rock-Rock.
Oil on canvas, 70×60 inches, 1966.
Dallas Museum of Art.
Gift of Mr. and Mrs.
James H. Clark.
Accession No. 1968.14

Elv the Pelv was aired originally only on black stations since no white folks sang like that back then. Mom twirled the dial to the far right where black-owned stations were segregated. "This is Daddy Deep Throat," the KYOK DJ intoned daily, hitting his highest register for "Deeeep" and lowest *basso profundo* for "Throat."

The first day KYOK played Elvis's *That's All Right Mama,* she drove 65 mph in our Olds 88 to buy his 45-rpm Sun record. Mama always beat the censors' ban which swooped down on airwaves and record shops faster than Bill Haley's Comet. She built a coveted contraband rock collection, starring Elvis.

Mother was probably the only Texas resident to have a complete set of shockeroos like the "Annie" songs by Hank Ballard and the Midnighters. Not *Annie* the orphan musical, not hardly. This was *Work With Me Annie* and *Annie Had a Baby.*

Kids flocked around the clock to our ranch-style house, like music junkies coming for a fix. While most parents forbade their children to listen to any rock 'n roll, much less the likes of "Annie" and Elvis, Mother would whisk the kids into our phonograph room where they'd become mesmerized. We all knew that if their parents knew, they'd ban their children from our home. My pride in having the sole cool Mama anywhere around was tinged with embarrassment, since I was at the pre-teen-queen stage.

On the day she discovered Elvis, Mother was burnin' when I got home from Oral Roberts Elementary School. "You've GOT to hear this." As she dragged me down our hall, I pondered superciliously—her new descriptive term for me—what in the music world could have transformed my highly-cultured, sophisticated mother into a schoolgirl. On hearing the first plaintive wails of Elvis, I knew.

We played *That's All Right Mama* over and over, flip side, back side, flip flop.

The doorbell began ringing with pals eager to hear the latest acquisition. Mother pried herself away from the hi-fi, opened the door, and left it ajar. Presley as Pied Piper. The gathering swelled, hours passed. Crinolined pre-pubescent girls and high-heeled, girdled matron alike were rockin'. The turntable wasn't the only thing overheating.

I couldn't have known during that first hearing of Elvis that no other musical event would ever affect me as much—except for seeing Elvis perform in the fleshy flesh almost twenty years later. By then, he was overripe but not yet decayed, and I was a seasoned reporter on a writing vacation in Las Vegas. The experience transformed me into a hunk o' hunk o' burnin' love. I was almost too excited to take notes, which never happened before or since.

Resplendent in that high-collared white suit trimmed with gold studs to match his reputation and his twenty-four-karat gold, jewel-encrusted karate belt, Elvis warbled disingenuously, "I'm not a king, I'm just a man, take my hand."

Women swarmed to the stage and shrieked, "Take my hand, take anything." Their upswept ringlets and bosoms bungeed like Slinkies.

I restrained myself from joining the throngs, but my traveling companion urged, "Do it, do it."

"I can't, I can't."

"Marsha, go on."

"I'm not a child. I'm a woman. I'm a reporter."

"All of the above," he reassured me.

Torn between his three-dimpled smile and Elvis's leer-sneer, I watched Elvis contract at the waist, bow out his tremulous legs, and croon, "You don't have to say you love me, just because you do."

"I love you, Elvis, I do," bellowed a woman at ringside. He bent down and kissed the screecher who grabbed the foulard from his neck. "Man, she meant it," Elvis said.

That triggered a stampede of be-gowned, be-jeweled middle-aged groupies who tried to scale the stage despite too-tight floor-length skirts or too-short minis. They strained to grab the sparkly panel of his bell-bottoms as well as his bottom.

Kid Galahad mopped his glistening chest with gold neck scarves and sweaty stuffed hound dogs which he flung periodically to the orgasmic fans. "Sorry, this is about as far as I can go."

At the finale, the king bent down again at stage front to grasp his supplicants' faces and kiss them. More hordes of females shook, rattled, and rolled down the aisles of the cavernous Las Vegas Hilton nightclub.

It's now or never, let yourself go, his songs cacophonized in my head. I never came so close to shaming myself, not while covering the Rolling Stones, Duke Ellington, or Luciano Pavarotti.

But I resisted sentimental me and scribbled final notes. I had been transformed and so had my luck. I gambled through the night and won back the two-hundred dollars I'd lost, plus some.

My article ran in dozens of papers, but *The Washington Post* created the best headline "Elvis: Writhing Revisited."

My stories earned a rare interview offer from his manager, the infamous Colonel Parker. I demurred, fearing transmogrification from reporter to fan. Besides, the only question I wanted to pose to Elvis was, "Will you sleep with me?"

Declining was a colossal mistake, of course. It would have been Elvis's only media interview during the last two decades of his life. I could have lived off reprint rights all my own life.

Exactly five years after that performance, the news of his death flashed across the radio. Immediately, I stepped out of my bath and gave Mother a condolence call. Bathwater and tears dripped down my skin as we commiserated.

I followed the call with a thank-you note to her for introducing me to Elvis, Verdi, Bix Beiderbecke, Mahalia—not Michael—Jackson, and so much more, from performing arts to civil rights. Above all, I wrote, thanks for the Elvis intro, "one of my best memories which so enlivened that era."

I did not mention a deeper connection: he always evoked a time when Mother knew best and loved me tender; long before her *Mean Woman Blues* made our beautiful home like a jailhouse, with only music to ease the heartbreak. I cut short many an argument by blurting, "Remember that day you discovered Elvis . . ." He was our Demilitarized Zone.

Throughout the years, Elvis remained a symbol of unity between Mother and me—even after her death. When I went through her few personal effects, I found my condolence and thank-you note. Pleased that she had kept it, I was instantaneously swept back to that magic moment.

The Elvis connection further eased lingering daughter–mother bitterness. I whispered, "That's all right Mama."

MARSHA DUBROW established an arts and entertainment beat for Reuters News Agency thirty years ago and has been writing about popular and fine arts ever since. She received a master of fine arts in fiction writing at Bennington College in June 2000.

EVE BAKER

Facets of Truth

I COME FROM ONE OF THE FAMILIES that have gone through the post–World War II holocaust crisis. The children at my Hebrew camp who had concentration-camp survivors for parents, my second cousin whose parents both survived (losing a son but finding each other again after the war), myself, favored grandchild of my Grandma—all of us whispering in the corner with the same enigmas and disorders in common. We've all had the same question to grow into: How can you live, when so many in your family are dead, killed at your age or younger, killed for no reason other than being in the wrong place at the wrong time and being from the same race as you?

IN MY HAND, THE STERLING SILVER TABLETS are small enough to be covered by a thumb. Pressing down, I can feel the Hebrew letters, engraved right to left across the split face: Yochevet Naftali, Zvie Hersh bar Zalman—the familiar shape of headstones—here lies mother and father. This coin-thin weight of silver, feeling heavier in my palm than the stone markers that are probably gone—razed or made into pavement in a Poland our family will never see again—is all that is real, along with a few unmarked pictures. . . .

"Dad, you're wearing Grandma's necklace. You're wearing it in the hollow of your throat, half unseen under your T-shirt; Dad, this is such a shock, frightening to watch you hang on to the tombstones just like Grandma. . . ." Then, you watch my face, only noticing my eyes on the necklace, not the tone of my voice, and you almost rip it off in your hurry to give.

"Evie, why don't you take it, you should be wearing it."

"No Dad, it's yours."

"You were her favorite. Grandma would be happy to have you wear it."

"Don't you want it, Dad? Don't you think Susanna or Alisa might get upset if I got it?" Though they now say I never did, at that time I tried each of my sisters: Don't you want it? Don't you want it first?" I really did say. And each backed away saying, "No, no, Grandma would have given it to you; she liked you best. That's good, you should keep it for all of us now."

So, I took the necklace, cautiously, honored by my father's trust, but uneasy about the implications of holding it too long in my hand or putting it around my own throat. After so many years resting on my grandmother's pulse, warmed with memories of her fingers rubbing around the silver edges, this feels too cold. On the back, I brush against "Layah" and "Yhudit" whispered and etched in a coarser hand, Leah and Judith, Grandma's best friends. Don't forget us in 1922.

We are not a grudging family, even though there were tussles over little items when Grandma died—a favorite candy dish, a brush and comb set that everyone had played with—the disputes had more to do with shock and the need for an object to invoke kind memories of this reticent, hunched little woman continually dressed in grey; no one has, truly, protested yet about me getting that necklace.

"No, I never said I didn't want it, " my middle sister tells me now. "Dad gave it to you without asking anyone else." She's crafting a monoprint of Grandma from her bridal picture, posed seriously beautiful in rich sepia shades; she's trying to remember Grandma's frown. "Dad never even tried to offer it to the rest of us; you'd better not lose it," she says.

This pendant that I hold so cautiously and hide so diligently in my sock drawer whenever I leave town is pure tradition, the favored European keepsake for those who, like my Grandmother Tamara Tashev, emigrated after parents died. She came over to America in her late teens: the treasured youngest daughter out of eight, the one who laughed and played practical jokes on her siblings. "No, the middle child," my father will say, pointing to a picture he's just found again. In it, Grandma is seated with her older brother and younger sister on either side. The child who knew nine languages, who had her high-school diploma stamped by the tsar (though my father now says this isn't true). She was the beautiful daughter who survived pogroms on her rich Polish family farm, then came to America on her way to Israel, and got dropped into her Manhattan world of sweatshops, sewing piecework during the day and scrubbing her relatives' floors at night. She's the one who wrote home the fatal words: "America is not paved with gold, don't come; America is not the land of opportunities, it is full of strangers and damp attics and poverty. You are better off at home."

Our cousin, survivor of the infamous Polish death marches and of watching her infant son being beaten to death, tells us over and over: "They never would have listened to her, I tried to tell her that when we got here. I told her that they never took her letters seriously. No one else *wanted* to come to America—she was the adventurous one, she was the traveler." This can't be true, my shrunken gray Grandma Baker who worried about going to the grocery store would not have been an adventurous traveler. "You see, we really didn't think this would happen. No matter how much they loved her, they were all very comfortable in Poland—they had the farm and the textile factory; besides, she was just a girl. Who would have paid attention to the opinion of a girl?"

Grandma married, to get away from her cousin slave-masters, we think. She married, had children, read the papers, and waited. This is, of course, only what I've been told; this is only what I've told others, what I've written about so many times that I'm not even sure what is real and what is only history. My father, at one time, said "Yes, this is all true" but now, getting older, he tells me: "No, Grandma never wrote those letters, Grandma married for love, Grandma chose to stay here—not go on to her boyfriend in Israel. She'd choose to stay even now."

Now everyone begs my sister for a print of the ghost impressions of her photography. My sister's Grandma is warm, sad, but serene in modified flapper pre-war bridal attire, a sepia bouquet of spikes: orchids and roses amid ferns, showy petals that clash in the bright colors of reality but mingle together sensuously in slow-timed photogravure black and white. Everyone wants this Grandma on their wall—not the continually stooped and worrying grandma who hovered in doorways, wondering all the time where her son was and why he only sent his wife to take her shopping; nobody wants the Grandma who would clutch the silver chain to her chest, whispering "I wish I was dead, I wish I was dead," who didn't even have to whisper anymore; we all knew what she was thinking by just watching her fingers press around the silver tablets at her neck. She could not find a good reason to be the only one alive.

"Nonsense," my father now says, "she loved you children, you were her joy, her eyes lit up around you. You had fun with her."

So, now I keep this pendant for everyone. I do not wear it, well not often, every time feels like an obligation. And what if it got lost? Generations of future family members, not to mention my father and sisters, might ask about it—what would I say then and how would everyone remember me? What could I make up? The careless youngest sister who lost the only tangible memory of our family's grave.

Facets of Truth

FROM EARLY ON, I WATCHED THE GERMAN FILMS on Kristallnacht with medical photographs of tortured Jews, mesmerized by the vitally alive proof on tape: the corded stacks of bodies; the naked women huddling above grave pits, terrified together. My own plump six-, then eight-, then ten-year-old body, seemed large to me in comparison, and I wondered for what side would I have been chosen—for work or death? How would my own flesh and frame have survived the cold, disease, and famine? As I got older, I started to wonder even more about the metabolisms of those who survived; did they come out—as a reward for their torture—thinner, stronger, and more capable? Or softer, wider, more unable to cope?

I played the fantasy war games children play: we're in the Warsaw Ghetto, Mila 18, and we can fight to the last, then kill ourselves; the SS are coming for my family, and I take a grenade, a Molotov cocktail. I run into the street and explode just as they begin to fire, and my family escapes. We're in a camp, and like my grandfather's friend who crawled under the rail cars at Treblinka, managing to warn his village before the next deportation (who didn't believe him and sent him back anyway), I would warn everyone, and this time they would all believe. We would all fight together and die fighting instead of by gas or starvation.

I fought my outdoor wars, lost tragically, died heroically, and then went inside to eat everything they could feed me: macaroni and cheese with ketchup, pepper steak, mystical combinations of broccoli and garlic.

How can you eat when so many people have died of starvation? My own grandmother lived on an old woman's diet of boiled eggs and cottage cheese. My parents had a freezer full of meat; they stockpiled cow.

I ate and threw up and ate and threw up—the magic of eating important foods, the pain of throwing up, and the absolutely fearless tired euphoria that followed this whole process made everything okay once more: I was pure, I was ready for battle, I was going to get there. Into this, I mixed a little bit of eastern Nirvana philosophy: I was going to become as pure as the air. I was not going to eat, to talk, to move out of position for hours, days, weeks at a time. And this would save me, give me a way to save the world, give me a way to not be afraid of death, to be able to stand torture more sturdily.

Dad, shaking his head, proclaimed: "You should have more Jewish friends; you should be able to look at a person and know for certain he is not going to betray you! How do you know that your goyische friend down the street won't turn you in? How do you know who is safe?"

At the same time, in a town where the Jewish population was nil, where in school the few Jewish kids I knew wore silver crosses and talked avidly of Christmas presents, as my parents built up their post-Depression post-War extra bulk food supplies and asked who would turn us in, my father also said: "So what's wrong with you, why don't you have friends; why are you sitting at home on a Saturday night reading books? Do you think you read too much?" He never understood how important I was finally being: that for once I was going to find a way of saving everything; I was going to never eat again.

Between my WWII pictures and my father's *Playboy* centerfolds, I had worked out both the equation and its definition: be thin. Thin people were superior, morally and spiritually, because to be thin meant that however much the world wanted you, you didn't care; that you didn't involve yourself in the sensual, somewhat tedious, and obligation-filled tentacled part of life; that despite relationships or yearnings, you were ready to go at any minute, to be tortured, to give, to be a good soldier for integrity and justice, instead of being the dragging-belly-to-the-ground, heaving slob who has held on to the illusion of life as it "should be" because she just loves pleasure—chocolate, good food, drink—too much not to be scared of death. Being thin meant exactly this: you were not scared. As I grew older, "thin" also meant that everyone fell in love with you and you got to have lots of good sex before you go.

Though neither Grandma (stick-thin herself), nor I, silently un-eating and suspicious of all people, was getting very good sex at the time, these two theories of starvation—both purification eating and the not-eating to be beautiful—still seemed to, quite rationally, combine. Think of this: if you can be very thin, then people will like you (not kill you rape you leave you kicked in the gutter).

Though, no, because look at the naked women in the photographs; very thin, stick-rib thin, but they all died anyway. So, perhaps if you're thin enough you won't care; or you'll look invisible, normal, like everyone else, and no one will pick you out as defective because your whole family is slated to die sometime in the future when someone whom you trust turns you all in and you—brilliant, beautiful, strong and thin—are able to slip past the guards and, in an athletic sinewy leap, holding grenade in hand, blow up the engine before the train begins to roll, saving your family once more.

Our family was, of course, slated to die if the Nazis came back. We were all heavy and slow and intellectual—made just to be slaughtered. Sure Grandma got out in time—just a fluke—she was meant to huddle naked above a pit, or die on the Polish death march, her pendant in a pile with the other junkier jewelry once the gold had been sorted.

EATING DISORDERS are generally associated with control of sexuality, with the way we look at beauty in this country, the demand on young females to be alike and unattainable; but, before anything else for me at nine-years-old, not eating or vomiting after every meal was literally a matter of choosing between life and death, or actually a matter of war. Here they were, my relatives in their camps, in their ghettos, humiliated, beaten, past consciousness, past dead thin—here I was in New Jersey with a big warm house and a full plate, preparing.

Shamans will sit on beds of nails, certain religious sects flagellate themselves for purification, masochists do the same for sexual ecstasy; but, beneath all these reasons, I've always wondered if the primal, main reason for self-torture is to prepare for being tortured by others—prepare to save yourself, to not give in, or give in only when it will be helpful. And how else does one make sense out of such tortured past histories?

So here is what, fingering this pendant and not looking too hard at my own stomach, I still seem to know about my Grandma and myself, and what I will do with this piece of my own history (even though my dad might say now that this is all wrong, too).

Grandma Baker—middle child, lone traveler to the new world—had a boyfriend in Israel, and she may have even had sex or at least kissing. After her parents died, America was supposed to be a brief stop along the way. Before the war started, before she left pogroms and many adored uncles and Leah and Judith behind, Tamara Tashev was also the family prankster—a joker with a great laugh—smart, beautiful, and certainly thin. Then, her family all died or were tortured and died. Only two survivors. And Grandma's husband suffered brain damage from a hold-up at his hardware store. After the hold-up, Grandpa, a former scholar, who couldn't walk anymore or read his books anymore or think clearly enough to understand his own half-mumbled sentences, kept whispering: "I wish I was dead, I wish I was dead, I wish I was dead." Then he died. And Grandma continued to clutch her necklace and whisper: "I should have died, I should have died, I should have died with them, too." Then she won; she died. And the war was finally over.

Myself? I am not thin, and I seldom wear my Grandma's coin-thin pendant—the weight of it slipping from my neck is too easy to imagine. But I keep the piece, and, when I go away, I hide it safely in a different sock every time. So, despite finally eating normally, despite finally staying alive, despite the final possibility of war ahead at any time, no one can say I lost our history on purpose. No one can say I never tried.

EVE BAKER says she is an itinerant writing instructor who spent much of the last spring hiking down the Appalachian Trail.

JAN FRAZIER

The Naming

I HAVE BEEN STEEPING MYSELF LIKE A TEABAG in the hot cup of remembrance, not just in rememberable things but in the unrememberable past, the huge one that contains all of my ancestors, known and unknown. Behind every person there is a web reaching back—an unfathomably complex network of imaginary lines, and for each line there is a name, whether or not the name is known. For every great-great-grandmother had her mother and father, and they had theirs, and so on, forever—if not literally forever, back beyond the time when people gave names to their children, or gave names to anything, or could even be said to be people, with the propensity or the capacity for naming.

One whose name I do have is Annie Lura Chamblee Frazier, whose body gave forth the small body that would become my father. She was dead at fifty, a year before my father would take a wife, whose body would not give rise to mine for eleven years. And so my grandmother has been known to me only through the telling of my father

Eugene Speicher. *Portrait of Andree Ruellan.* Oil, c. 1945. Oliver B. James, Phoenix, Arizona, April 1952, Arizona State University Art Museum, Tempe, Arizona.

(though his time for telling ended many years ago, for he died at about the same age as his mother, when I was eighteen).

I have this photograph of her, my grandmother young and beautiful, her lacy white collar high beneath her chin, and in that one picture her eyes are uncovered because still seeing. In all my other pictures of Annie, taken in her later years, her eyes are invisible behind dark glasses. I don't know if she wore them because the light hurt her, or if her blind eyes were, she felt, unlovely to those who still had eyes to see.

She had long hair like I had, when I was a girl, and I wasn't a very big girl before I understood the connection between those two things—that my father missed having long hair to brush, and so of course his daughters would wear theirs long and thick like waterfalls down their backs. He told us stories of how his mama would sit on a low stool on the porch of the old farmhouse, and she would draw hairpins from her thick black braid that wound twice around her head, the braid unlooping like the coils of a heavy rope tossed down from a ship. He, my boy–father, would sit behind her, and with his fingers, callused from picking cotton, would unravel the three ebony strands from one another. Annie's hair reached very nearly to the porch floor, and my father would brush it, following the path of the brush with his other hand. His mama would hum, just the way she would sing sometimes, sitting in her wheelchair, strumming her lap harp. Her voice carried out to the cotton field, where my father and his brothers worked with their pa under the hot Mississippi sun, their backs bowed. The pointy seeds pressed into their fingertips, sometimes tinging the fluff pink. Their mother's voice kept them at it. She had, my father loved to say, a beautiful voice.

There is a picture of my sister and me in the pink kimonos our father brought us from Japan. Our backs are to the camera. We are sitting on the living room floor, facing the TV, which is off. Our hair has been brushed and brushed and lies in waves down our pink satin backs, and it just touches the rug, falling below the broad obi tied at our stick-figure waists. I'm pretty sure that picture was Daddy's idea.

He was on a ship when she died. He was with his brother Lamar (who would be blown to bits several years after on a different ship, a kamikaze casualty). The cable came from their father saying that the multiple sclerosis that had blinded and crippled her had finally undone her. My father and uncle—not yet my father and uncle—could not leave the Pacific theater to go home to bury their mother with her black hair all around her. My grandfather put Annie in the cemetery on Red Hill.

They are all of them now in that rich, warm clay: my grandfather alongside her, Lamar (for his remains were recovered from the water and shipped home), and his sisters and brothers—save my father, who is buried in Florida sand with my mother. I have stood before all of those tombstones and copied down the dates, come home to Massachusetts and attempted to make order of them, to place myself in a particular history.

Steeped in all of this, I have been sitting nights at the computer inputting known data into my genealogy program and searching the web—the one strung across cyberspace—to see if I can fill in some blanks. The other night I was entering dates when my daughter stood beside me to say good night. She—the beginning of the web reaching out in front of me—put her hand on my shoulder and said, "Good night, Mama." I kept my hands on the keyboard and stretched up to kiss her cheek but then suddenly was made—as if by a force separate from myself—to get up. I stood, put my arms around my child, and held her close to me, where she wanted to be. Then I came to understand there were more than two of us there, for Annie Chamblee, sure as life—substantial and strong as a cup of well-steeped tea—was holding Laura too. It was as if my grandmother had slipped inside me and said, *Now you get up out of your chair and hold that child, while you can.*

"Good night, Mama," Laura said again and began to take her arms from around my waist. I could feel Annie's arms inside my arms around my daughter, her great-granddaughter. I felt myself, too, being held by the woman that once held my boy–father.

I whispered into Laura's hair, "No, wait, just a little longer. Let me hold you another moment," so she turned her face to my nightgown and let herself be held by us both and let her long hair be stroked down her back.

When I got into bed myself a while later, Annie was still with me. I lay in the dark, aware of her presence as very nearly a physical thing, and after some time I said to her, "What shall I call you?" I didn't know if when she was alive she would have been called "Grandma" or "Nana" or what—if there had been a grandchild to name her when she was still on this earth. I have always thought of her as just "Annie." Now, with her so very present, I needed to know by what name to address her. But there was no answer, only her enduring presence, and the tangible experience of being loved. That was enough. Annie stayed until I grew sleepy, and then I felt her go, and I slept—tucked in, grandmothered at last.

JAN FRAZIER is a poet and an amateur genealogist. She is presently working on a memoir.

ANGIE PELEKIDIS

The Wedding

I COULD BECOME THE FIRST FEMALE PRESIDENT of the United States, regain the other half of Cyprus for Greece, and win the Nobel Prize, but nothing would make my parents happier than if I married a Greek. Of course, this is because they are Greek and are proud of their heritage, though neither can name a play written by Euripides or an essay by Plato. It also didn't help when my older and only sister, Georgia, married a man who was half-Italian and half-Irish, and therefore a mutt in my parents' eyes. I then became Ma and Daddy's last hope to maintain a one-hundred percent Greek bloodline. Now, had I been born a Golden Retriever this emphasis on pure bloodlines might have been more relevant.

Part of the problem was that when my parents immigrated to America in the mid-fifties, the Cleaver family was the ideal and *Father Knows Best*, and I tried to live up to these standards. I won them a gold medal in the Offspring Olympics they had going with their Greek friends and relatives by getting my doctorate in English. Then they could brag about their daughter, "Dr. Deonosopoulos."

However, as a result of my unmarried state at thirty-two, the prestige of this medal decreased. After my thirtieth birthday, hints about the type of person I should marry became less subtle and more frequent. "Wouldn't it be nice if you met someone and got married?" became "Wouldn't it be nice if one of my children made me happy by marrying a Greek?"

Not that my parents ever asked me about my love life. According to them, I didn't have one because I was still "pure." I never contradicted them on this because there was no middle ground with them: an unmarried woman was either a virgin or a whore. My father had an analogy for female virginity which originated in his growing up in a military family (his father had been a major in the Greek Army): according to him, virginity was like a rifle. Every now and then when I

Opposite:
Will Barnet.
Woman and Tall Trees.
Oil on canvas, 1977.
Farnsworth Art Museum,
Rockland, Maine.
Gift of the artist, 1991.
©Will Barnet/VAGA,
New York, New York.

spoke to him on the phone, he would tell me in his heavily accented English; "Remember, if you shoot off your rifle, you lose the war," the war, I guess, being marriage. Ma preferred American analogies: "Why buy the cow when you can get the milk for free," the cow, I guess, being me.

Which explains why I never mentioned to my parents that I had been with my boyfriend Sam for the past three years. It hadn't been as difficult as it might seem because they had retired to Florida and rarely came up to Bay Ridge, Brooklyn, where my sister and I lived. Then Sam and I decided to get married, and my only thought was how was I going tell my parents I was marrying a Chinese-American man.

I attempted to tell Ma about Sam after we had been dating for a year and called Florida with the sole intention of doing this. Her first question was the inevitable: "Is he Greek?"

"No, he's not, and I don't think you'll be too happy with what he is," I hinted, thinking this would be enough for her to change the subject. Ma has the sensitivity of a bloodhound when it comes to detecting the unpleasant. This can sometimes work in your favor and sometimes not, like, if your funds are low, and you're hoping for an extra generous birthday gift. You'll start the conversation by saying how broke you are, and she'll scent the approaching request and start talking about how broke she is.

"Oh no!" she had said in her heavily accented English. "He's a Jew!"

"No Ma, he's not Jewish," I had replied. "He's a half-African-American, Irish-Muslim from Turkey." I knew she'd pass this on to my father who was, as usual, listening to her side of the conversation. For years he tried to teach Georgia and me to hate the Turks, but it was impossible for either of us to relate to the Ottoman Empire or Cyprus.

My mother laughed loudly over my creation. "Costa, Alexa is going out with a black Turkos!" she said, translating it in Greek for my father and leaving out most of it. "Oh no!" he said in the background. This is how most of my conversations with Daddy take place, with me talking to Ma on the phone and him making comments in the background to whatever he understands from her side of the conversation. This means I can hear all of his cutting remarks and criticism, but he can't hear any of mine because my mother refuses to relate them to him. And like the chorus in a Greek play, he always has something to say. Once in a while, he picks up their other phone and talks directly to me. Then they'll start arguing with each other, and it's almost like being there. Daddy says in Greek he's only trying to make me perfect, and Ma tells Daddy in English that she doesn't need a Philadelphia lawyer, a saying I have never understood.

So three years passed, and I never told my parents about Sam. I knew what they would say about my marrying him. When they realized I wasn't teasing them, and after my mother's calls on the Virgin Mary to intervene, and my father asking me if I was crazy, they would bring up the two most important reasons why it was a mistake: what people would think and my destroying their dream of grandchildren that were full-blooded Greeks. The marriage would also nullify all of my Offspring Olympic gold medals and thus place me so far behind that nothing would ever regain me the lead.

Sam and I decided we'd introduce him to my parents at the wedding of one of my pseudo-cousins, which was taking place in Brooklyn. My parents were driving up from Florida, and Sam and I were making it our first event as a couple on my side of the family. Though Ma and Daddy knew nothing about Sam, he had heard stories about them from me, Georgia, and my brother-in-law, Frank, and was probably dreading the meeting as well.

I spent the weeks before the wedding imagining how it would go. At best I'd get one of Daddy's sayings that sounded absurd when translated into English, something like you braided the rope now go hang yourself with it. I knew they'd try to make me feel bad about choosing such an occasion to bring Sam to, but my thinking was that having all the relatives and strangers who spoke Greek as well as English on hand would prevent my father from saying anything nasty.

I'm sure my brother-in-law Frank felt it was about time someone else was the foreign spy in the Deonosopoulos camp. With Georgia and Frank attending the wedding, I could count on having two allies present though there was always the possibility Georgia would remain neutral. My sister never seemed to defend me as strongly as I defended her to our parents, maybe because she was tired of hearing so much about Dr. Deonosopulous and never anything about Mrs. Frank O'Brien. But then, my mother was also a master at pitting the two of us against each other. If she was mad at Georgia, she'd call me and say, "Your sister says your apartment is a pig sty," in the hopes I'd say something bad about Georgia. I'm sure she did the same thing to Georgia when she got mad at me.

My parents were, as usual, staying at my sister's house while they were in Brooklyn, which I preferred to having them stay with me. Regardless of how clean you keep your house, Daddy will find fault with it, and in my case, the biggest fault was my dog Shem. I knew Daddy would never stay with me again after his first visit to my apartment. His nose had wrinkled in disgust over the dog food bowl in the kitchen and the dog bed in the living room, and he had sat on the edge of my couch as if avoiding contamination. Afterward, he told my sister the couch smelled like Shem, and that the dog hair, which he said was everywhere, got all over him.

Strangely enough, Daddy had gotten me Shem as a puppy eleven years earlier, an act completely out of character for him since he says the only good animal is the kind that provides food like a chicken or a cow. He swears he got Shem for me because he was afraid I'd pay money for a purebred dog, which to him would have been a sin. Since then, he's never stopped trying to convince me to get rid of Shem. For years I've had to listen to the same speech, half in Greek, half in English: "Do you still have that darn dog? Why you still have him? Why you need to have animals? They tie you down. Who's going to marry you with that darn dog? Get rid of him," which sounds more like "Getreeddaheem" the way my father says it. When I know I'm going to see Daddy, I prepare myself by mentally repeating that over and over again.

I slept poorly the night before the wedding. I dreamt Daddy was trying to throw Shem down a well, and Georgia, my mother, and I were trying to stop him. In the dream I called the police and could hear the sirens approaching, only they didn't sound like normal sirens. I woke to the sound of the phone ringing. I let the answering machine get it because I knew who it was.

"Alexa, are you home? It's your mother, call me at Georgia's," she said in English. It was 7 AM. My mother believed that because she needed only four hours of sleep, the rest of us could survive on that too. When I called back she answered Georgia's phone.

"Hallo," she said in her overly loud and cheerful voice.

"Hey Ma, what's up? When did you and Daddy get in last night?" They had driven all the way from Florida because my father was too cheap to fly. He had probably done all the driving too, because my mother felt it was the man's job.

"We got in at after midnight and stayed up talking to your sister until 2:30. I called you before, were you sleeping?"

"Yeah Ma, that's what people usually do at 7 AM on Saturdays."

"Oh, I'm sorry, my baby. I only slept three hours. Come over for coffee."

"Ma I can't. I've got a ton of stuff to do this morning."

"Fine, you don't want to see your mother?"

"Ma, that's not it, but I've got a ton of stuff to do."

"Alright, alright. I miss you my baby! Do you still look beautiful?"

By no stretch of the imagination could I ever be considered beautiful. Attractive, maybe, on a good day, but beautiful, never.

"I'm alright, Ma. I'll see you later. Meet me outside the church."

"Okay. I love you, my baby."

"Me too, Ma. Bye."

I don't think I've ever heard Ma call Georgia her "baby." My parents don't deny I'm Ma's favorite while Georgia is Daddy's. Ma accepts me as I am, while Daddy tries to make me into a replica of himself, a mini-Costa.

A little after 1 PM, Sam picked me up, and we drove to the Greek church on Colonial and 84th. I wondered if Marie Antoinette had been as careful with her appearance before facing the guillotine as I was with mine. Not that any special pains I took would make a difference, because it would all melt in the heat. It was one of those still days in the middle of July when sweat beads on your upper lip the moment you step outside. The church where Georgia and I had been baptized and where my parents had gotten married sat on the ridge that had given Bay Ridge its name, and if there was a breeze anywhere in Brooklyn it would be here.

Sam double-parked across the street so I could look for my parents, and I quickly spotted them on the church steps standing by themselves. From the car, I could see Daddy's six-foot tall, mostly thin frame in one of his thirty-year-old suits he couldn't button over his large stomach. It was too hot to button anyway, and I wondered how long the wide blue and grey striped tie that didn't match the dark brown suit would last around his sunburnt neck. I saw him wipe the sweat from the top of his large, mostly bald head with what appeared to be a dishrag. I was surprised he hadn't tied the dishrag around his head. According to my Thea Aggeliki, who lives in the same development as my parents, Daddy sits in a chair outside the house all day with a rag tied around his head, chain-smoking, and looking like a "Turkos."

Ma had on the dress she had worn at my sister's wedding. It was dark mauve with three tiers that began at the waist and ended at the hem above her knees. She and Georgia had similar bodies, stereotypical Mediterranean figures: short—my mother was only five-feet-tall and my sister five-three—with large breasts. After two kids and many years, my mother's waistline had almost entirely disappeared. I had taken after my father and was tall and thin. It was an old saying in our family that I had gotten the brains and Georgia had gotten the breasts. I knew Ma had her hair done that morning. It was perfectly feathered back from the front of her face to form a crease down the middle of the back that Daddy said made her look like she had an ass on the back of her head.

She looked tan and healthy, and I knew she had been going to the beach regularly. She ignored the skin cancer warnings in the media. When I spoke to her about it, she waved me off as though the scientific findings of my generation didn't apply to hers. It was part of an unspoken competition between Ma and her two oldest girlfriends as to who looked the best. Ma would comment on how badly Thea Stasia's face had wrinkled ("Like a fig"), though she was still so darn thin, or on how heavy Thea Loula had gotten, though her green eyes were oddly free of wrinkles ("A face lift, for sure"). Then she would ask me in her heavily accented English, "Your mother still looks good, eh?", which had only one possible answer.

"Toula and Costa are the two by the door on the far left," I told Sam, pointing them out. "The short, plump (or, as my father would say, "fluffy," a term of high praise in his unique vocabulary) woman in the pink dress with the glasses and blonde hair. And the tall man next to her in the dark brown suit who's bald." Sam nodded when he picked them out. I hoped seeing them would lessen his anxiety. They didn't look intimidating.

"You ready?" Sam asked me. I shrugged and moved to open my door.

"Let me get that," Sam said, stopping me. He opened his car door and got out, walking around to the passenger side to open my door. The slamming of his door had gotten my parents' attention, and they stared in our direction. From where they stood, they couldn't see Sam's features clearly but could probably see his long black hair held back in a pony-tail, which was more than enough reason for them not to like him. I loved his hair, the strong line of his jaw, and the molded contours of his cheekbones. I loved his voice with its heavy Brooklyn accent. After more than three years it still hurt looking at him.

He opened the door and took my hand. "You're being gallant today," I said.

"I'm trying to make a good impression," he said, still holding my hand as we crossed the street to the church.

"You shouldn't bother," I told him, dropping his hand when we reached the church steps.

"My baby!" my mother said, coming down the stairs to hug me tightly. Part of the irony of her calling me her baby is that I stand almost a foot taller than she in my heels. "You're late," she said in Greek, a look of surprise and dread on her face when she noticed Sam. I heard her mutter in Greek when she pulled away from me, "Mother of God, she wants to kill me." My father was shaking his head in disbelief and contempt. I thought how much Sam must love me to put himself through this.

"It's my fault we're late," I told them in English, translating what Ma said for Sam. They spoke Greek in front of people who didn't understand it to exclude them. "Ma, Daddy, this is Sam Wu. Sam, this is my mother and father."

"It's a pleasure to meet you, Mr. and Mrs. Deonosopoulos."

My father ignored Sam's outstretched hand though my mother nodded and said hello. She was being polite, trying to maintain a middle ground between how Daddy would want her to react and how I would. I saw my father wince when he heard Sam's last name.

"Everybody's already inside. We've been waiting outside for you and roasting for an hour," she said in English.

"We're barely late," I said. "Why didn't you go inside if it's so hot out here?"

"I wanted all of us to go inside together like a family, but I ask too much."

"She went to get Chinese food," Daddy said sarcastically in Greek.

"Be quiet Costa," Ma told him in Greek. "Don't start outside the church."

"Sam's got to find a spot, so we'll meet you inside." I didn't want Sam to have to walk into the church alone, but he shook his head at me.

"I'll find you inside," he said.

"You're sure?"

"Let him go," my father said in Greek, "and tell him not to come back."

My mother told him to be quiet again and ordered me to follow her into the church. I kissed Sam quickly on the lips when they had turned and did what my mother told me.

It was dim and blessedly cool within the entrance of the church. The ceremony had begun, and I could hear the chanting and singing of classical Greek, which unlike modern Greek, I don't understand. The ceremony sounds Middle Eastern, though my father would argue with this because God forbid you should associate anything Greek with the Middle East. The deep voice of the priest was joined by the higher wailing of the male church singer.

At the far left of the entrance hall was a high rectangular table covered in a deep-red cloth with dozens of white candles on it. A gray-haired man in a pin-stripe suit with dark circles under his eyes stood behind the table. The candles were arranged by size and price. Placed in the center was a basket with money in it. The man smiled and greeted us in Greek as my mother walked over to him. She chose three of the largest candles and placed a twenty in the basket, much more than the cost of the candles. My mother liked to give people the impression she was wealthier than she was, and could certainly afford it here since she went to church maybe once a year.

"What about Sam?" I asked.

"Do you see any Buddhas in here?" my father asked sarcastically.

"Shush, Costa," my mother scolded him. "Get him one later," she whispered to me.

She handed us our candles, and we walked to one of two long, narrow wooden boxes on either side of the central door leading into the main area of the church. The boxes were filled with sand into which were embedded lit candles in varying stages of melting. I lit mine off one of these and stuck it into the sand. With my right hand,

I did my cross. On either side of the central doorway and between the sand-filled boxes were two icons, one of the Virgin Mary and the other of Christ. I walked to the gold-embossed, glass encased Virgin Mary to the left of the door and once again did my cross before leaning over to kiss it without actually touching it with my lips. It was covered with lip prints in several colors—pinks, reds, and browns.

Ma watched me closely as I did this. She held out her hand to me, and we walked behind Daddy. He sat immediately in the first pew to the left of the doorway on the bride's side. There were at least ten empty rows of pews between the three of us and the rest of the guests.

"Costa, why are we sitting here?" my mother asked loudly in Greek.

"So your daughter doesn't embarrass us," he said, handing her the rag to put in her purse.

"If I'm such an embarrassment, I'll sit somewhere else," I said in English.

"Costa, be quiet," my mother said, and squeezed my hand in warning as she pulled me with her to sit down. Still holding my hand, she kissed me on the cheek, no doubt leaving an imprint of her lipstick as on the icons.

"My baby, you look beautiful," she whispered loudly and with pride in Greek. It occurred to me then the real irony of her calling me her "baby" was that I was thirty-two years old. When I was with my parents, I often had to remind myself of this.

"So do you Ma. You look thinner." She didn't, but I knew she'd like to hear me tell her so.

"I don't eat anymore. I worry about my kids too much."

Daddy began to say something in response to this, but she silenced him with a "Quiet Costa, don't start here" and a look upwards at the stained-glass dome in the center of the ceiling that depicted the Resurrection.

"So, what do you think of Sam?" I asked her.

"Not now," she said in an undertone with a subtle gesture of her eyes to Daddy.

My mother pointed behind me, and I turned to watch the three bridesmaids walk down the aisle. Their blue taffeta gowns looked like something Scarlett O'Hara might have worn. The hoops under the skirts caused the dresses to rub against the pews, making a swooshing sound in the otherwise quiet church because Greek weddings don't have music, just the priest and church singer. In their left hands, the bridesmaids carried folded-up matching parasols, and they wore large floppy hats in blue tulle. In their right hands they carried large bouquets of white flowers with long blue ribbons trailing from the stems.

I felt a nudge at my side and turned to face my smiling mother. Her glasses were perched low on her nose, and she looked over their rims at me. "You like the dresses?" she asked me.

"Take a guess," I said.

Looking at the people in front of us, I spotted my Thea Loula, mother of the bride, in the first pew. Her husband of thirty years, my Theo Georgos, had died a couple of years ago. Once, when I had met her for lunch at the diner where she waitresses, she told me she'd never been in love.

I've always wondered about Ma and Daddy's relationship. I know she loves him, but the closest he'll come is to say with a shrug, "I'm used to her."

"Thea Loula looks good," I whispered to my mother.

"She gained weight," Ma loudly whispered back, "but her face looks good. You see the man next to her? He owns the diner she works for. His wife is dead."

"I think that's great," I told her. "It's ridiculous how some Greek women put on black when their husbands die and never take it off."

"Your mother's going to do that for me," Daddy said over Ma's head, teasing.

"Don't be too sure, Costa," she said. "Quiet now, here comes Stephi."

I turned to watch my pseudo-cousin, the bride. Her brown hair was in a knot at the top of her head with wisps of it framing her face. A small wreath of white rose buds encircled the knot, and she held a bouquet of white roses in her left hand. Her gown was the required white with short sleeves, a tight waist, and a full skirt. Stephi's right hand was curled around the left arm of a short bald man, her future father-in-law since her father was dead. When they reached the altar, he kissed Stephi's cheek and gave her hand to his son.

Sam and I were planning on a small, simple ceremony the following June. We were going to get married in the Greek Orthodox Church just for tradition's sake and hopefully to appease my parents.

I began to wonder where Sam was, though I knew it was hard to find parking around the church. I wouldn't have blamed him if he had gone home.

"So what do you think of Sam?" I asked Ma yet again.

"Why you ask? You sleeping with him?" she asked, hoping to surprise me.

"Ma!" I was extremely good at feigning shock and indignant innocence. "Of course not! What do you think I am?"

"Good," she replied with satisfaction.

"Well, what do you think of him?" I knew I was pushing it, but I wanted to get their reaction, to get it over with.

"He's Chinese," she said, as if there was nothing more to say.

"No kidding? Really?" I said. Daddy shook his head in disgust.

"None of you could make your mother and me happy and be with a Greek," he said loudly. "See how your cousin made her mother happy by marrying one? Aren't you proud to be a Greek?" he asked me over my mother's head. I noticed some people sitting in pews in front of us turn to look. Their presence would keep me from yelling, but not my father.

"Yeah, but I can't marry somebody just to make you happy."

"Why, haven't we done enough for you?" he asked.

"So I'm supposed to marry someone I don't care about, just to make you happy? Please, like you made Yiayia happy by marrying Ma. Ma was never good enough for her."

"And look how I pay for that," he said in Greek. "At least your mother was not a Chinese."

I noticed a couple more heads up front turning to look at us.

"All right Costa, don't shame us in the church in front of our relatives."

"Me shame us? Your daughter is shaming us."

"I'm going outside to wait for Sam," I told my mother. I got up as quietly as possible to leave, but my mother's loud whisper to come back was easily heard. I heard her say something to my father, and his angry reply of "too bad."

I walked outside the church. The heat and brightness of the day was intense after the air-conditioned and dim interior of the church. I walked down the first tier of steps and sat down. There is something about Daddy's anger that almost immediately brings tears to my eyes. It's part fear, though he's never hit me, and part frustrated anger. Just once I wanted to tell him to mind his own business and shut up. I heard the door open behind me and knew it was Ma. She always chases me down when I fight with Daddy. She sat down next to me and handed me Daddy's dishrag, which I childishly pushed away.

"You shouldn't have walked out like that. It looks bad."

"Would it have looked better if I had sat there arguing with Daddy?"

"Why you pay attention to him? You know he's only teasing you."

"Ma, you know he means everything he says."

"You know your father and me want only what's best for you."

"Please. You know he wants to be able to brag his perfect daughter married a Greek."

"What do you want me to say? That your father is terrible and hates you? That he wants you to live a miserable life? Alexa, he's your father, and you can't change him. He's done a lot for you." She waved at a fly that had come from nowhere and was flying slowly in front of her face. "After all these years you still don't understand him." The fly flew drunkenly past my mother's face only inches from her mouth, and I was caught between watching it and her. "If you were smart, you could have him wrapped around your fing . . ." She didn't get the chance to finish the last word because she had inhaled the fly.

I watched speechlessly as she made a sound like a cat coughing up a furball and spit the pieces of the fly into my father's dishrag. I tried not to laugh. I wanted to be righteous and angry. I dug my nails into my palms and bit the inside of my cheeks, but it was futile. I began to giggle hysterically, my eyes tearing up now from laughter.

"Oh, you think this is very funny. You laugh." Ma was furious at me for laughing at her, which only made me laugh harder. Maybe her anger was comical because I wasn't afraid of her.

"Go ahead, laugh. I remember that, Alexa," she threatened as she got up, but she wouldn't—unlike Daddy, who remembered everything and seemed to base how much he loved me on whether or not I did what he wanted.

"Ma, Sam and I are getting married," I told her in a rush.

"For sure, you're trying to kill me," she said, stopping before going inside and only briefly looking back at me. "We'll talk about this later."

"There's nothing to talk about," I said, but she had already gone inside.

A few moments later, Sam walked up the church steps and gestured with an envelope, our gift to the couple.

"We forgot this at your apartment," he said. "Why are you out here?"

I gave him my hand, and he pulled me to my feet. "I got into a fight with Daddy, walked out of the church, and watched Ma swallow a fly."

"I missed all that? Wish I could say I was sorry."

"I told Ma about the wedding. It's not going to be easy," I warned him as we walked back into the church holding hands, and this time I wouldn't let go.

The daughter of Greek immigrant parents, ANGIE PELEKIDIS was born in Brooklyn. Though she has lived in Long Island, Florida, upstate New York, and Alabama, she always returns to Brooklyn and currently resides there. She received a bachelor of arts in English literature from St. Lawrence University and began working on a master of arts in the same field at Auburn University. Realizing she wanted to write English literature and not teach it, she switched to a more practical degree in mass communications. After graduating she returned to Brooklyn to work in public relations in New York City and has been the Public Affairs Manager at the New York Aquarium for the past year. She reads literary fiction that has withstood the test of time and will soon begin studies for a master of fine arts in creative writing.

DONALD L. ROSE

If Winter Comes . . .

WATCH SMALL CHILDREN AT PLAY. Listen to their exclamations and laughter. Do the same with young people, adults, the elderly. Who is having the most fun? Try asking a child about the desirability of a life without the toys and games of infancy. Older stages of life may not sound as attractive.

Emanuel Swedenborg, however, suggested that the time for the most fun ("delight" would be his term) is old age. Think about it. You might say, "I don't want to be an old person with aches and pains and illness." Of course, illness and pain are not fun at any age. Swedenborg was referring to the quality of delight:

> If one will consider, one will know that every age has its delights and that by these he is introduced by successive steps into those of the age next following; and that these delights had served the purpose of bringing him thereto, and finally to the delight of intelligence and wisdom in old age (*Heavenly Treasures*, no. 4063).

Swedenborg's thought reveals an interesting brand of optimism about life. The delight of the present is a stepping stone to something better. I can remember the delight on Christmas day when I was a young child. The time when we opened our gifts was sheer joy for me. Now I am a grandfather, and although I am less excited about what might be in the package with my name on it, I experience deep delights at that special time. My childhood joy was like a sweet tune played on a single musical instrument. These days I am enjoying something more like a symphony orchestra. I know that Swedenborg was not just talking about family celebrations. What do you suppose he meant by the delight of wisdom? Perhaps that is a gift yet to be unwrapped and appreciated in celebrations yet to come.

DONALD L. ROSE, son of a newspaper columnist, is co-editor of *SPI (Swedenborg Publishers International)*. He also edits a monthly church magazine, *New Church Life*. He and his wife Noelene live in Bryn Athyn, Pennsylvania, and have five children and three grandchildren.

REBECCA A. HALL

What Could Be Better?

Max Pechstein. *Sonne am Ostseestrand.* Oil on canvas, 1952. Collection of The University of Arizona Museum of Art, Tucson. Gift of Edward J. Gallagher, Jr.

IT WAS FIFTEEN YEARS AGO that my husband said, "Come with me. I've got something to show you." He was and has remained a man of few words and infrequent demands, so without questioning him further, we—he, I, and our daughter—packed into the cab of his truck and ended up at a boat dealership on Pacific Avenue in downtown Tacoma.

Inwardly, I moaned. A boat. I don't swim. I fear the water as much as I crave to be near it. Then, there was the child issue. In my role as Worried Mother, I foresaw the four-year-old going overboard, me diving in after her, both of us fighting white-capped waves as my husband tried to shut down the engine and throw us life-rings, ropes, or seat cushions.

"What do you think of her?" he'd said as his hand caressed the sleek fiberglass.

I held the daughter's hand tighter.

"It's—nice," I said. "I like the color."

He nodded. "Like brand new, too. One-hundred-twelve hours on her and only two years old. The owner died of a heart attack after he'd taken her out a couple of times and now his wife's ready to sell."

I thought about curses, about buying other people's misfortunes. I looked at our daughter, who'd broken free and was hanging off a ladder from the back of the boat, her tennis shoes churning the air.

"Nineteen foot Bayliner," a voice beside me said.

It was a salesman.

He and my husband skirted the boat, talking horsepower, bilge pumps, inboard/outboard, Volvo engines, sleeping capacity, weight, and ease of launching.

I corralled the child and diverted her by looking at fish in a saltwater tank near the manager's office. Behind us the male voices continued, broken by pauses followed by clicks and thunks as the boat apparatus was demonstrated.

The daughter lost interest in the fish tank and ran to the ladder of the boat again. She struggled to pull herself up to join her father, who was checking out the engine compartment. He lowered the cowling, leaned down, and pulled her up to join him. Now it was the three of them inspecting the boat—the nineteen-foot-like-brand-new-Bayliner boat.

"Hey, Honey. Come on up. I wanna show you something."

I thought, Where have I heard this before?

I looked at his face, at the anxious arch of his eyebrows, the hesitant smile, and I knew then that this was important. Unlike some men who dream of owning a sportscar or a motorcycle with a high-powered, window-rattling engine, my husband wasn't and isn't a man who aspires to the trappings that others might hold dear. But this boat was something he really wanted. Something he would willingly share with me and others who might ask, but in fact it would be his domain. A floating island where he answered only to himself or maybe didn't answer at all. A raft that could free him from shirts and ties, telephones, and cars. A place where he could be soft and empty.

I climbed the ladder and planted my feet in half expectation of a nonexistent wave.

I edged past the salesman, brushed against my husband's back, looked at the daughter, whose hands were clenched around the steering wheel, her mouth making motor noises.

I asked, "Where's the bathroom?"

The salesman looked at my husband, who smiled. "I'll buy one."

"What?"

"A portable potty. Put it right up there." He pointed toward the bow, to the narrow vee between the bench seats.

"Right out in the open?" I asked.

This got the daughter's attention. "But everybody will see us."

The salesman laughed. My husband smiled bigger. I raised an eyebrow.

"The front is mostly covered so you could duck down, and it'd be private."

The salesman nodded.

The daughter was satisfied with the proposed arrangement and resumed revving her imaginary engine.

I looked at the space between the seats, mentally calculating the proportions of a portable commode. When I looked back into my husband's eyes, I knew that I held all the power. I could end this dream with a shake of my head or by climbing back down that dangling ladder.

Hours later, back at home, the daughter played with her kitten. Her chuckles grew into whoops and hollers as the kitten leaped for a ping-pong ball as it bounced off the lid of the new portable potty, complete with enzymes and biodegradable toilet paper.

MY HUSBAND REMAINED DEVOTED TO HIS BOAT for six years. From spring to late fall, every weekend, he would rise before the sun and dress in layers that grew heavier with the seasons. Without much early morning appetite he would spread peanut butter on bread, grab apples, a bag of chips, and four beers before he'd leave, boat in tow, to meet my father, his fishing soulmate.

At first, it was hard to imagine the two of them alone together without my mother and me along to suggest, question, or object. But they managed fine without us.

My father would meet my husband at the Point Defiance Boat Launch, a place serene and green where the late morning bustle of boats and people would chafe the much-sought-after solitude. But earlier, at 4:30 AM, it was a silent, personal place where my father and my husband, two men I love more than any I've ever known, would go to the boat launch and back the trailer into the cold water of Commencement Bay.

My father contributed bait, helped with launching fees, gas, and extra beer. Just-in-case beer. In case it was a warm day. In case they caught a lot of fish. "Those salmon can be real toughies to land, you know. All that work can make a person pretty thirsty."

He also brought chocolate bars—Hershey's Milk Chocolate or Cadbury Fruit and Nut. He said they both went well with beer.

I have no idea what these two men in my life talked about on their morning excursions. They never said, and I don't recall asking beyond, "Catch anything?" They always did. Sometimes it was only a Ling cod, a rock fish, pollock, or dogfish, those shark-like creatures that sink like dead weights on the end of a line and strip bait from hooks with abandon. And often, they would catch the prize. The Cohos and the Kings. Those beautiful, full-bodied salmon with powerful tails that move against the currents, who are tempted by a flash, take a greedy gulp and feel the awful tug. They're fighters, these fish, with a will to live that exceeds their capacity to think or feel. It's that powerful will that fishermen say is what makes the salmon a challenge and a joy to catch.

My mother and I never went with them. While they said we were welcome to come along, they would invariably look at each other and one would say, "But we're launching at 4 AM." And the other would say, "Well, be sure to wear your woolies because it's pretty darn cold that time of the morning." So I knew, and my mother knew, we would be imposing. It wouldn't be the same for them if we came along. Maybe they'd have to be mannerly with women on board when all they really wanted to be was just "guys"—to pee over the side of the boat, belch if they needed to, or launch a string of curses if a fish broke the line or got tangled in debris.

So Mom and I, with the daughter in tow, went shopping instead. We gossiped, laughed, tried on clothes, and had lunches at restaurants with white table linens. We were satisfied that we were having much more fun than our spouses.

Later we'd find them. My husband asleep in his recliner, fish scales flecking his too-small sweatshirt, his whiskers bristly from being—oh joy—unshaven. My father would be asleep on the couch, lying on his back, hands behind his head, mouth open, a bit of belly showing. They would both be snoring. The television would be turned on to some athletic event. They probably stayed awake only long enough to see the score. They were like men well stuffed from a good Thanksgiving meal. But there had been no turkey, no potatoes, no pie, only fresh air, comraderie, a few beers, and the hunt for the wily salmon.

It was lovely. They were funny and sweet, and now I see how quickly that time has passed by.

The twosome parted when my mother became ill. During the last two years of her life my father was her careful nurse and staunch soldier. There was little time left for recreation.

I think my husband was lonely for his fishing companion. He asked friends to come along on the boat, but he never asked them a second time. I consented to go, but only at a later hour—one past that magical twilight time when fish and the men who hunt them begin to move deliberately and with purpose before the light of day reveals their secrets.

In the ensuing years, my husband's job has taken us from Washington to Texas, and then to far away New Hampshire. My father has stayed behind, moving from the western side of Washington to the eastern side, building a life without my mother.

Although there have been other fishing trips, with other companions, in different locales and different boats, I don't think it has ever been the same for either of them.

These days my husband and father speak only from a distance on the telephone. From time to time they reminisce about how they used to navigate the whirlpools under the Tacoma Narrows Bridge where remnants of the original bridge, "Galloping Gertie," lay where it fell more than fifty years ago. They talk about the time they docked in Gig Harbor for—yes—a beer and watched as a well-dressed lady misstepped and fell into the bay. They remember the Orcas that once came through a group of boaters. How everyone cut their engines, pulled in their lines, hauled up their downriggers and sat in silence and awe as the black and white behemoths rolled like waves among the boats, their eyes surfacing, blowholes spraying as they passed.

They still talk of going fishing together. My father dreams of going to Alaska to fish the clear waters for salmon too large to hold with one hand. But I don't know how it could happen. The years have made him frail, and the alliance with his son-in-law has grown more distant with time. I feel an urgency to fulfill my father's dream, to help him relive moments of buoyant joy. But maybe, just maybe, the memories are enough. Maybe nothing could be better than what was.

I have a picture of my father and my husband, standing side by side dressed in bulky rain gear, boots, knit caps, holding in each of their hands a salmon as long as their legs; on their faces are smiles.

They are two boys free of responsibility. They are best friends up to no good. They are brothers in agreement about the importance of salmon fishing. They are father and son, not by blood, but in spirit and respect. And most of all, they are mine.

REBECCA A. HALL lives in North Carolina where she is working on a Vietnam-era novel. Her husband has not resumed fishing; however, a few times a year, her father drops a line into Lake Coeur D'alene.

KEPPEL HAGERMAN

Surry County

In the spring
when dogwood spread its white lace,
I'd go with Mama
to the place she called
the sad country.
I never asked her why,
I only knew I didn't like it,
but she wanted company.
She'd sigh and stare
at empty houses, half-burned buildings,
chat about people who used to live there.

Always on Confederate Memorial Day
we'd lay a flag on Grandpa's grave.
Mama would tell me about others in the family plot,
Baby Abner, age four months, Ida, age sixteen,
siblings she never knew.
I'd grow restless, long to start home.
After I was grown and far away,
Mama wrote she didn't go to Surry anymore,
it made her blue
to see the weeds take over.

Now on a day in another spring
I drive my grandson to the sad country.
We find the cemetery buried in weeds,
hack away at chokeberry, scuppernong vines.
Noisy crows fill the sky,
their wings darken the horizon.
Almost sunset, the wind rises.
Patrick shivers, asks when we're leaving,
asks why I bring him here.
I say it's a place you need to share
with someone you love,
that if he keeps coming he'll know.

KEPPEL HAGERMAN was born in Richmond, Virginia, and graduated from Duke University. As a Navy wife she taught English in Seoul, Korea. A poet and short-fiction writer, her most recent work is "Dearest of Captains," a biographical narrative poem about Civil War nurse Captain Sally Tompkins.

PART III

Roundabout

WILLIAM KLOEFKORN

Star of the East

I stand with my sister near the altar
at the front of the sanctuary
singing Star of the East, O
Bethlehem's star,
guiding us on to Heaven afar.

It's Christmas Eve. The church
smells like dry fur on the collar
of an old heavy coat. My sister, she's

an angel if there ever was one,
with her right hand
squeezes my left. To reach the high notes
she closes her eyes: O star
that leads to Heaven above . . .

My sister is my mother's daughter, and
I am my mother's son—Mother,
who couldn't carry a tune
in a sack, nonetheless
singing a tune each morning
as she filled the sacks—a sandwich,
an apple, a wedge of cheese the color
of a Kansas sunrise.

It's because my sister is my mother's daughter that
she must close her eyes to reach
the high notes, and it's because
I am my mother's son that
I must return the squeeze of my sister's hand
to reach the low ones. Eventually
this song will end, its sweet discordances
going the way of all that's born
of breath and tongue. Eventually
Santa Claus will burst
like an obese miracle red and white
into the sanctuary, where eventually
he'll remove the burden from his back
to distribute sacks of candy
to the children, I and my sister
among them, we two meanwhile

singing our jittery little hearts out,
Heaven no more above than below,
Heaven in the hands that fill the sacks,
Heaven in the notes both high and low,
Heaven in the act of being here
alive together
singing.

WILLIAM KLOEFKORN'S most recent collection of poetry is *Welcome to Carlos* (Spoon River Poetry Press, 2000). The state poet of Nebraska, Kloefkorn writes and teaches in Lincoln. The photograph shows Sylvia Shaw, a Chrysalis author and University of Rhode Island English professor, with her cousin Enrique long ago.

FORSTER FREEMAN

To the Center and Back

Cindy A. Pavlinac.
The Cretan Labyrinth
Mendocino County,
California. Photograph,
Cindy A. Pavlinac, Sacred
Land Photography.

THERE WERE SOME SURPRISES IN STORE when I first walked a labyrinth several years ago. There still are.

After I had composed my spirit and reverently entered the designated starting point at one side of the massive circle, my anticipation was that I would smoothly follow those beckoning graceful curves laid out on the floor until arriving unremarkably in the middle. That was my first misconception. Although unfamiliar, the designated pathways laid out in front of me felt congenial, inviting, encouraging in the first few turns back and forth, back and forth. "Yes," I supposed, "just disengage your mind and saunter peacefully along these uneventful ways to the goal."

Then arose the first awakening. Having progressed from one side's perambulations over into the other half of the circle, it seemed I was mostly there. How simple. Simple until the lines carried me all the way back to the first side again so that I found myself quite disoriented from my initial concept, without comprehension of how this design was going to guide me, noticing this was not in my control. Ah-ha—that must be part of the scheme inviting me to detach from my conceptions! Only surrender. And trust. There is some higher wisdom behind this design. Abandon yourself to the adventure with glad expectation.

"This is your life journey," something said inside of me. So *that's* what this ages-old piece of art is for. Not amusement—well, some of that, too, and whimsy. No place for smugness. Not total detachment from the rest of the world's people, as I was periodically made aware that I was walking this with several other persons, occasionally passing or brushing by one of them. Not predictable, yet not chaotic either. No, there was a mystery here that kept calling me onward, a journey with some holy meaning. Keep on toward the goal. Keep awake; don't miss a thing. Pause for a moment. Be as free as you can. Try letting your body swing. Step backward awhile; sideward. Perhaps be a pilgrim traveling on your knees. Carry with you a prayer, a question, a deep desire, a willingness for revelation, a smile. The meaning is not exclusively in attaining the center; it's also in learning how to pursue the journey. Experiment, make choices. Go with awareness always—the reminders of issues in your life, the questioning, the weight of sadness, lift of joy, noticing a fellow-traveler, acknowledgement of a gracious presence, perhaps unseen companions—now childlike, now offering a deepening commitment, striding purposefully, filled up with compassion, abandoning again.

It's true my living goes like that. Doesn't yours? I read today that St. Gregory of Nyssa "was a man enchanted with Christ and dazzled by the meaning of his Passion." When he was twenty, he was inspired to begin engaging in church ministry. Then he pulled back, preferring instead a career as rhetorician like his father. Along came his imperious older brother Basil, who compelled him to become the bishop of Nyssa. Perceiving himself to be unfit for such a position, Gregory later described the time of his ordination as the most miserable day of his life. Nonetheless, he negotiated the turn and stayed the course, meaning to be faithful in whatever he was dealt within God's providence. When he attended the Second Ecumenical Council in 381, he was honored as the "pillar of the Church." He became one of the three eminent Eastern theologians now known to us as the Cappadocian Fathers.

I look back over the twists and turns of my career and see again that every major change came as a surprise to me, every one unwelcome at first. Now celebrating fifty years of ordained ministry, I give thanks for each of those turns in the path. Knowing about Gregory bolsters my courage and joyful resolve to follow where they take me.

No wonder walking the labyrinth was an archetypal devotional practice that attracted and nurtured believers in all religious traditions around the world in ages past. Its re-emergence as a way of trysting with the Holy One in the recent decades of our head-heavy western world is a mystical gift suited to encourage/hearten/inspirit us who aspire to life as pilgrimage.

The inviting form that is being laid down lately in churches and gardens and retreat centers—with stone, woven carpet, inlaid wood, paint on portable canvas, plant materials, even traced with masking tape on a wood surface, sometimes with wide tracks for wheel chairs—is usually copied from the one laid in the floor of Chartres Cathedral in France around 1220. The primary impetus in the United States radiates from the Grace Cathedral Labyrinth Project, in San Francisco. Our Trinity Episcopal Cathedral in Portland, Oregon, where Julia and I worship, has inlaid a labyrinth into the hardwood of its fellowship hall in handsome curly maple, American eastern cherry, and rosewood (signifying Mary and the feminine).

Only after the Chartres design was established within the cathedral foundations did the walls begin to soar from it to their Gothic heights. This became one of the seven Pilgrimage Cathedrals of Europe. There are no tricks or dead ends here, as in a maze; only a single path drawing onward the person who desires that the eye be single. Eleven circuits of the path are enclosed in a circle divided into four quadrants, forming the ancient Celtic cross. These are the same sections of quaternity, representing successive states of spiritual development and the union of pairs, as are seen in the points of the compass and the quarters of heaven, the elements traditionally believed to compose the physical universe, the arms of the cross of Jesus, the Garden of Eden with its four rivers, the four beasts envisioned by Ezekiel, Daniel, and John, which also depict the Evangelists of the Gospels, and the New Jerusalem coming down from heaven.

In the concept of Carl Jung, the four-quadrant circle is a *mandala*, using a Sanskrit name. Viewing it, meditating on it, moving within it suggests to the inner mind our moving on the path of integration, wholeness, self-realization, with all the disparate parts of our makeup held together around the center and protected from the outside by the enclosing circle. Many consider the most remarkable *mandala* in the world to be in the Buddhist tradition: the enormous Barabudur in Central Java, probably from the ninth century, built around a hill, with the characteristic four gates and intricate walks. Some of the very earliest Christian churches were constructed on this pattern, notably St. Vitale at Ravenna in the sixth century. Variations on the basic design are found in drawings preserved from prehistory, and in the dreams of primitives and modern sophisticates alike, as their godly knowing awakens.

Tread faithfully and lovingly the winding paths of your labyrinthine search, and you are certain to find yourself one day at the center. Some call it the road to Jerusalem. Some associate it with the three-fold mystical progression of purification, illumination, union. The twisting, frequently discouraging, journey of ego-shedding leads to what is experienced and described in a multitude of ways. What is found at the destination is the jewel, the child, the flower, the flame, the seed, the city built on a rock, the priceless pearl, the center of being. It is the Christ at your center. It is the real self and the authentic identity of the human community.

The representative image encountered where the physical labyrinth's track reaches its fulfillment is an open circular space containing a seven-fold rose design: an entrance and six connected petals. It is a space in which to pause, rest, pray, recollect, contemplate, give thanks, and integrate the gifts of the journey inward.

This is followed by the journey outward. Traverse your way back over the same path by which you came. Carry with you an insight gained, a strength granted, a love newly kindled. You do not tread the path of discovery and transformation for yourself alone, nor are you permitted to remain contented in passivity. You are blessed so you can be a carrier of blessing. When you arrive again at the opening by which you entered, breathe anew a prayer of thanks that you can be used purposefully and go about your adventurous calling.

A good attitude for leaving the labyrinth was suggested to me in a recent time of Ignatian style prayer. I had read in John 13 the story of Jesus washing the disciples' feet. Then I visualized myself as one of those in the circle of disciples, feeling reluctant to have my Lord minister so to me and at the same time yearning for it. "Feet," I said to myself, "are what connect me to the earth, what keep me upright on it as a human being, what propel me on the journey appointed to me in this world. How necessary it is for them to be both strong and pure for progressing on the way."

I had a brief dialog with Jesus about feet and washing, about my resistance to his serving us who are to be servants. I told him I had a desire to walk in a way that would attract others to him. What most surprised me was his response. He said to me, "The more I purify you, the more others will notice my gait in the way you walk."

FORSTER FREEMAN is a semi-retired spiritual director, teacher, and ordained minister of both the Presbyterian Church (USA) and the United Church of Christ. Holding a doctorate in ministry in Spiritual Direction from a Jesuit seminary, he has taught in eleven summer sessions at Roman Catholic institutions. He and Julia moved four years ago to Portland, Oregon, to be closer to children and grandchildren. He is the author of *Readiness for Ministry through Spiritual Direction*. Forster currently serves as president of the Swedenborg Foundation Publishers.

KAREN EVERSON

A Magical Tradition
Neo-Paganism

THE SLOW RHYTHM FROM A SINGLE DRUM called us out from the forest. A full moon in the midnight heaven turned mackerel clouds into a skyscape of silver and star-flecked indigo. Under the night sky we formed a circle. A man holding a torch came forward. We were gathered, he said, to celebrate the night of Samhain, the turning of the year, to honor past generations who had gathered for thousands of years beneath the stars to celebrate the continuing wheel of the seasons and to rejoice in life.

As he spoke, I glanced around the circle. The thirty-odd men and women who stood illuminated by moonlight could indeed have been a gathering from a thousand, or five thousand, years ago. Under the ageless moon within that sacred space, we were becoming a single being, encompassing all times and all places. In the center of our circle the torch was set to a tall cone of branch and tinder; the fire blazed up, and the drum throbbed with a fresh and more urgent life. Joined, we danced three times sunwise around the circle, then spun off like sparks to dance and leap the flames. Our bodies became celebration and sacrament, and we danced the fires to cinder and ash.

I knew that night that I had found something I would never willingly relinquish. Moonlight and sacred fire had entered some dark center of myself and had stilled a lifetime's yearning. In that transforming center I had found magic, and since then I have considered myself a part of the philosophical and religious movement of Neo-Paganism.

Georgia O'Keeffe. *Blue and Green Music*. Oil on canvas, 57.2×47 cm., 1919. The Art Institute of Chicago. Gift of Georgia O'Keeffe to the Alfred Stieglitz Collection. 1969.835. Photograph ©2000, The Art Institute of Chicago.

There are as many varieties of Neo-Paganism as there are of Christianity—perhaps even more, since there are large segments of the Neo-Pagan population who firmly resist any attempt to define dogma or create a priesthood, pursuing instead a personal gnosis, an intimate and personal relationship with the divine. It is therefore difficult, if not impossible, to make any definitive statements that will apply to us all. However, the sense of a magical universe and a magical self is a vital part of the lives of many, if not most, Neo-Pagans.

Like most of the traditional Native American religions, many belief systems encompassed by the term Neo-Paganism hold some concept of magic as central to the spiritual and functional life of the individual. Magic is a fundamental concern for the best known and perhaps largest Neo-Pagan movement, Wicca, and other Goddess traditions, as well as for Celtic-inspired systems such as modern Druidism or the Celtic Faerie Tradition.

The term magic has been so diluted over time that its common present meaning barely suggests the power and awe the word originally conveyed. For this reason many Pagan writers sometimes use archaic or "odd" spellings—magike, magick, magyck—to suggest the original, wonder-filled meaning of the word rather than the more modern sense of legerdemain or sleight of hand.

Magic, in this deeper sense, is believed to come from the transforming center of the soul. It depends on the concept of a fabulous, divine, or semi-divine realm within the mortal world. The mind and heart can both perceive and touch this sublime aspect of reality. Such touch and perception can exalt and change us, and can also, it is believed, influence and change the world around us. "Magic" is how the sacred touches and changes us, and how in turn the individual participates in forming and creating the reality of existence.

Perception may best be described as a continuing sense of wonder and a willingness to be surprised by the common beauties of the senses. The perceptual ability to find the fabulous, the mythic reality that underlies physical reality, is a vital part of the Pagan spiritual life, since it is this vision that transforms physical and emotional events into the experience of the magical and divine. Magic as the act of influencing material reality is thought to be a combination of perception and will, often aided and shaped by ritual.

Use of the trained will is the second essential aspect of most magical belief systems. Pagans believe the human mind—the will—can affect the body and the material universe. An ill person, for example, who believes in recovery and who focuses attention and energy on healing will recover more quickly and thoroughly than by thinking of the illness as chronic and centering on the disease. Medical science would seem to support this contention. Many Pagans believe that the whole purpose of the interaction of the divine and the material worlds is to allow people to be agents of beneficial change. No individual can—or should be able to—control reality. But many of us feel that we grow as human beings—as souls—only when we try to be active agents for good in the world we share with our fellow beings. Thus a Pagan also directs energies to the benefit of others.

Ritual may be used to assist both perception and will. Religion, even secular life, is full of ritual, and Neo-Paganism makes varied use of it. Even spontaneous ritual invests events with a memorable specialness, whether of solemnity or joy. We all have a store of memories we may think of as "magic moments."

In terms of creating transforming magic, ritual is used to enhance awareness of the sacred and to bond a number of people to a common purpose. Sometimes elements of ritual—the use of chants, music, incense, herbs, or other materials—is mistaken for magic itself. These things are only tools—"magic" is a thing of the soul. A sacred symbol may evoke a sacred thing—indeed, many symbols of commonly celebrated holidays go back to early Pagan religions. Evergreen boughs that symbolized the persistence of life through the cold darkness of winter have become the Christmas tree. The Easter bunny was once the sacred hare nurtured by Celtic tribes as a symbol of fertility and whose well-being could auger good fortune for the community.

There are no "magic words," only words which help the worker evoke magic strength, or connect with others who have performed, or are even now performing, that same ritual, reciting those same words, celebrating that same purpose.

The celebratory ritual described at the beginning of this article, for instance, was intended to increase and enhance the perception of timelessness and transcendent joy essential in the seasonal rites of Paganism. A similar rite, however, could have been used to raise the magical energies of a group, which would then be focused to some good purpose. The purpose might be microcosmic, as for the healing of a member or a friend, or macrocosmic—a kind of magical prayer for religious tolerance, for peace in a troubled region, or for the preservation of our ecology and the survival and well-being of our fellow creatures.

The function of ritual is to remind the magician of the dual nature of reality and to allow the practitioner to function both in the fabulous, magical universe, as well as in physical, everyday surroundings. The Pagan must keep a foot in each world, understanding how each affects the other. Work must be done, not just in the spiritual world, but in physical reality as well, according to one's means and abilities. A pagan who works magically to support, for instance, the environment, needs to work in the "real world" as well. Not everyone can drop routine responsibilities overnight to join Greenpeace, but most people can recycle, and there is a host of useful actions in between. By being aware of the sacred that underlies everyday actions, daily experience becomes a soul experience, each event assuming its proper perspective and importance in the light of both everyday and spiritual reality.

To lose awareness of the sacred is to risk disconnection from the first and best source of love and hope. To abandon the secular, material world, however, is to lose the ability to do good in that world. Such disassociation from material reality is not the way of the mystic or the holy person.

The magical self transforms and shapes the reality of the worldly self through the revelations and strength of the spirit. This understanding and knowledge help to put the irritations of mundane life into perspective, releasing energies for creativity, for teaching, for healing, and for love. To recognize one's own strength, to recognize one's own capacity to make a difference in the world for the good, and to help this recognition bloom in others is to bring the greatest of magic into reality and to experience the fabulous as the most profound of truths.

I WROTE THE PRECEDING ELEVEN YEARS AGO. Rereading it with an eye to updating it, I found myself regarding my younger self with affection and some amusement. How earnest I was! How terribly serious! And how very committed to my "true path."

Is my true path still true? Oh, yes. I am still a priestess, still a woman of magical perceptions. But where, eleven years ago, I would have described my spiritual life as being like my blood, hot, coursing, giving animation and passion to everything, now I would say it is more like my bones, holding me strong and steady in the currents of my life. Without going into details, let's just say I've had need of it from time to time. It hasn't kept me safe from sorrow—nothing will do that except a numb and indifferent heart—but it's been both something to cling to and a guide-rope back to joy.

I'm entering menopause—a little early to be croning, but I'm comfortable now with the role of wise woman, even when I haven't always been able to be wise for myself. My magic hasn't turned my hot flashes into power surges, but it does keep me from worrying much about aging. I like the woman I am, and the one that I'm becoming. There are still times when I am overwhelmed by the sheer wonder, the magic, of the world—the greening grass stirring under my soles, the heartbeat of the earth in my blood, the sudden, unlooked for blessing of a cardinal's song or the sight of the first snowdrop. Though perhaps I'm a bit more subtle in my approach now, I still teach others to find strength and beauty and joy in themselves.

One of those I try to teach is my own daughter, Caitlyn, now seven. I'm not involved with a group right now, and my private rituals are intimate and quiet. Currently, the aspects of my beliefs I share with Caity are mostly those of attitude and ethics: kindness, compassion, allowing others the freedom of their beliefs without necessarily holding them yourself. I've overheard some interesting conversations, especially as Caity has had a few evangelist Christian playmates. "When you die, you go to Heaven or Hell," one five-year old friend declaimed. Familiar with her mother's belief in reincarnation,

Caitlyn looked up, politely interested. "Really?" said my daughter. "I thought we got recycled."

We talk a lot. I sorrow that, at seven, Caitlyn has a few classmates who are already parroting the language of hate—sometimes racial, sometimes religious, sometimes anti-gay. "Mom, what is sin?" she asked. "Sin is hate," I tell her. "Sin is hurting someone else, deliberately and without cause. Sin is believing that someone else is evil just because they're different."

I am a Neo-Pagan priestess; I am also a mythographer, student of the history of religion. All religions, at the last, boil down to the same essential truth: treat your fellow humans with decency, respect, even love. What differs, through history and even today, is who your religion—or your immediate society—defines as your fellow man. So I teach my daughter to be a priestess to her own connection to the divine. Listen to your compassion, I tell her. Listen to your heart, your conscience. Don't let anyone tell you that hate is right, or good.

When she was four, my daughter asked me, "Mommy, what religion will I be when I grow up?" So many things went through my mind. I remembered the drum calling me out from the forest, the glory of the night, the sense of being one with creation as I danced the stars down. I remembered the rush, the incredible fiery feel of magic flowing sole to fingertip, I remembered the sublime peace of private worship, and I wanted all those things for her, my daughter. I thought also of my husband, partner, and mate for twenty-two years, who is an agnostic and secular humanist and one of the finest, most moral and ethical people I have ever known. And I thought, reluctantly, that Caity seems to enjoy her occasional visits to Grandma's orthodox church.

Any path can be valid if you follow it with love and tolerance. "You can be whatever religion you want," I told her. "As long as you're a good person."

"Okay," she said.

Later that night I came upon Caity, dancing joyously to silent music amidst the flowers and the moonlight in my temple, and blowing kisses to the moon. I watched in secret for a moment, then left her to her own innocent communion. Whatever outward shape her spirituality may take in days to come, I dare to believe that the center will hold true.

KAREN EVERSON has a master of arts degree from Ohio University in ancient cultures and creative writing. She has published one novel, *The Last Voyage of Odysseus*, and manages Moongate Designs through which she distributes her artwork, poetry, and other writings. She is a priestess and teacher within in the Pagan Community.

PAT SCHNEIDER

Uneasy Alliance

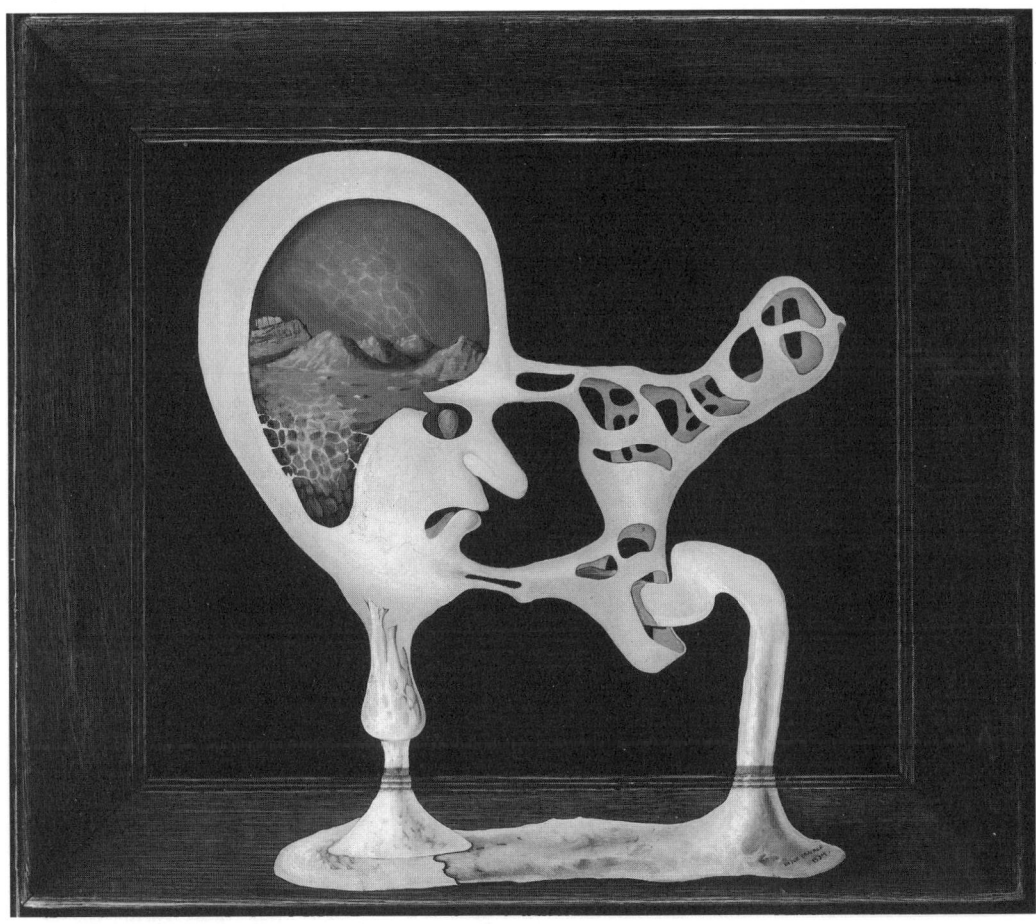

Victor Brauner. *The Turning Point of Thirst.* Oil on canvas, 50.5×59 cm., 1934. The Art Institute of Chicago. Promised gift of Mr. and Mrs. Joseph Pulitzer, Jr.; restricted gift of Richard Gray; Alyce and Edwin DeCosta and The Walter E. Heller Foundation Endowment. 1992.652. Photograph ©2000, The Art Institute of Chicago.

There was that porcupine
that my child tried to pet.
There was that huge snapping turtle
that I tried to move off a highway.
There was that wild turkey no one moved
in time. There was that jackrabbit
we hit on the desert and found
still stuck to the car's front grill
a hundred miles farther west.
There was that falcon's silent swoop
between branches above my small,

leashed dog—how the great bird
stood on a branch and considered.
How the little beagle sniffed a trail
without apparent concern
that it was on a falcon's mind.
There was that snake beside the bike path,
its face frozen into ice at the edge
of a tiny, temporary pond.
How I jiggled it with a stick,
how it awoke, broke free, fled,
and left an imprint of its head in ice.
There was that mourning dove
at the bird feeder, eating seed,
and then the peregrine, eating
the mourning dove.
There was that old, old man

from Cambodia. How he pushed
a grocery cart, gathered bottles and cans
from the neighbor's trash
for redemption.

PAT SCHNEIDER is founder and director of Amherst Writers & Artists and its press. Author of plays, libretti, and six books, including three volumes of poems and *The Writer as an Artist: A New Approach to Writing Alone & With Others* and *Wake Up Laughing: A Spiritual Autobiography,* Pat has been featured on National Public Television and Radio for her work with writing workshops designed to empower low-income women.

RAE HALLSTROM

The Age of Addiction

BOB REMOVES HIS GOLD WEDDING BAND and hides it beneath a chocolate candy-bar wrapper in the map well separating the bucket seats in his green pickup. It is the last thing he wants to think about. He inhales smoke from an expensive, imported cigar and chugs the hard caffeine rush from a can of Classic Coke. While stopped at a traffic light, he funnels a shot of rum into the metal pop-top hole and swirls the can to mix it. Without thinking, Bob detours from the grocery store and winds up in front of the Osaka Health Spa.

His body also on auto-pilot, he strolls in the front door and threads his way to the clean but dented reception counter. The Korean-born proprietress has seen better days. One of her cheeks is swollen, but she smiles at Bob as though he is the King of Siam. The usual fantasy unfolds. He is invincible—stronger than muscle-bound men half his age, smarter than his boss's boss, as much a superman as Clark Kent. In her eyes he sees the unabashed lust of animal instinct, and it is easy to believe she is aroused. Together they retreat to the spa's inner recess.

An hour later, Bob pushes an overflowing cart to the grocery checkout. He places the Honey Nut Cheerios, bananas, ground chuck, and Pampers on the conveyor belt and crosses the last item off the list. He hands the cashier the coupons that his wife has carefully clipped. It is not until he pulls his wallet from his back pocket, that he remembers the cash is gone. The clerk scans his Visa and waits for verification. He is so high he has forgotten that he is over the credit limit. Bob is about to come down and come down hard, not because he abuses nicotine, chocolate, caffeine, and alcohol, and not because he's irresponsible with money, spending family funds on

selfish pleasures. The core reason why Bob is in trouble, is his long-term debilitating addiction to sex. Bob is a sex addict, but like the society we live in, Bob hasn't come to terms with his problem yet. Neither has the woman who serviced him.

BILL'S SITUATION IS ARGUABLY DIFFERENT. He prides himself on the fact that he's never had to pay. A professional with a high-profile position, he struggles with alternating cycles of humility and grandiosity, egotism, and low self-esteem. The exception is his silent boyhood promise. When he watched his stepfather beat his mother in a drunken rage, Bill vowed he'd never drink to excess and never strike his wife. Long ago he resigned himself to the fact that he is blessed with a high libido. What he's doing is only natural and, he rationalizes, it's not even sex in the strictest sense.

Sometimes he wonders how he managed to go so far—a beautiful wife, educated and successful in her own right. A daughter who never had to see domestic violence, or fear for her safety. And in business, well, he's at the peak of his career, and he won't go down without a fight. Of course, now that she knows, it pains his wife, but she has to cut him some slack. He puts in long hours. He deserves all the gusto he can get. Though he admits to having some regrets, Bill's a passionate man and carousing revs his engine. He sees no reason why he ought to stop. Not that he couldn't quit, cold turkey, if he put his mind to it. But why should he?

It's not as though sex is a drug. It's not that he's breaking the law. It's not even as though he's the only guy who gets some on the side. So, even while his opponents relentlessly dog his every escapade, he generates more ammunition. Intellectually, he knows his behavior is not without risk, but this is not an issue of the intellect. He has urges. He has needs.

THE MOTIVES AND MIND-SET portrayed in the preceding exemplify what may be the most disquieting form that addiction is known to take. In addition to shame, financial woes, and the potential for violent and legal consequences, sex addiction breeds distrust in that most intimate of settings, the marital bedroom. But that's not all. Sex addiction also threatens a family with venereal disease and unintended pregnancy by adultery. These are not victimless crimes.

Addiction has plagued humankind for centuries, yet this is the first era of progress in reducing the power of the addictive cycle. From Alcoholics Anonymous, established in Akron, Ohio, in 1935, to the many spin-off Twelve-Step groups, people have been helping each other find sobriety. Fifty years ago, alcoholism was considered

Opposite:
Paul Klee. *Mask of Fear [Maske Furcht].*
Oil on burlap, 39½×22½ in. The Museum of Modern Art, New York. Nelson A. Rockefeller Fund. Photograph © 2000 The Museum of Modern Art, New York.

a moral flaw. AA pioneered a process that not only helped people overcome the problem, but helped them and others accept the alcoholic's behavior as a disease. By practical application, AA proved that the symptoms of the body are connected to ailments of the spirit and mind. In time it is very possible that the symptoms appearing in addicts will be seen for what they are: manifestations of the failings, excesses, and other ailments of individuals, families, and society as a whole, and that recovering addicts will become healers, able to illuminate our cultural blind spots.

Non-addicts serve as co-dependents for addicts; that is, they enable the addicts to continue in their destructive behaviors. They do so in many ways that none of us completely understands, but partly by making jokes about self-destructive behavior, instead of admitting to broken hearts, by denying wounds instead of listening, by requiring abstinence amid exponential increases in temptation, and by insisting that they have no part in this problem, instead of realizing that we are linked in many ways, some of them not at all obvious.

Like an ecosystem, the whole of humanity is in an equilibrium of sorts, and within the equilibrium are the functional and the failures, the haves and have-nots, and the addicts and non-addicts. While choice will always play a factor in the personal outcome, few knowingly choose to suffer.

Our very lifestyles isolate us. We aspire to flourish all by ourselves, as little islands of independence, self-determination, and individuality. To what does a man or woman turn in the pursuit of life, liberty, and pleasure? Because, when being lovable is in doubt, liberty essentially does not exist, and life brings little pleasure.

The first semblance of a life raft becomes a substitute for warm feelings, like the fuzzy blanket that Linus, the Peanuts cartoon character, clutches. It becomes the substitute lollipop, the substitute binky, the substitute love that few got enough of. What is the life raft? Whatever flashes a facade of euphoria, that is, instant well being and membership in the club of success. Whatever promises to be predictable, reliable, and relentlessly pleasurable, even if in a decadent, sinful, or self-indulgent way. Some dull their pain with another kind that can be controlled. There is not one answer, but many. We have become islands, and on a fundamental level, we are not the least bit happy about it.

Addiction is as varied as human nature. Aside from alcohol, people have become dependent on narcotics, nicotine, and caffeine—all unnecessary, toxic foreign substances, unlike food, exercise, or sex. "Comfort foods" is a phrase that evokes instant recognition, because most of us indulge in something—chocolate perhaps, or pizza—on occasion. It's easy to understand that food can be addictive in excess, after all, gluttony is one of the seven deadly sins, but then, so is lust.

It's becoming easier to recognize intentional deprivation, including anorexia and bulimia. Yet food is still a physical substance, and one that is ingested. Exercise and sex are natural functions of the adult body that can result in healthy highs. Of these, sex is far more likely to become addictive, because nature tempts us with an intensely pleasurable experience and possibly the high of all highs.

Other activities can become addictive, such as gambling, working (the workaholic), churchgoing and praying, cleaning, shopping (the shopoholic) and often with it shoplifting or overspending. What these varied substances and activities have in common is that they feel good and take up time. Not just any time, but time that would otherwise be spent solving or resolving life's problems. Whether stimulant or numbing agent, addictions fool us into forgetting whatever it is that hurts. They cloak reality in fantasy.

There is a deep hole in many addicts, a hole they seek to fill with either substance or activity, and the more often they avoid looking into the hole, the larger and darker and more frightening it becomes. This hole is a wound caused by the belief that, when stripped of the mask forged to fit into society, in the deepest core, the addict is unlovable. All is not right in the addict's world. While the logical course would be to confront the source of stress and pain, without help the addict almost never chooses this path.

Worse, the neurological pathways for every step of the addiction become entrenched. It is easier to repeat learned behaviors, no matter how complicated or painful, than to forge a new path. And, because memory is physically encoded in the brain, repeated behaviors are more difficult to change than a one-time dalliance. Practice does not always make perfect—it tends to make permanent.

This is the Age of Addiction because so many of us are addicted to so many different activities and substances. But it's also the Age of Addiction because it is possible to see an end to the madness. Just by talking about addiction we help to curb its appetite. By labeling addictions we shine a light on them and make it more difficult for people to use them to hide. Through anti-drug programs in grade schools to new approaches in therapy and the proliferation of Twelve-Step programs, we are a culture that is beginning to face our culpability in this addiction craze. Recalling John Donne's "no man is an island, entire of itself," we should take heart that the cycle of pain can be dealt with lovingly and effectively by reaching out to humanity with compassion and awareness.

RAE HALLSTROM began her career as a journalist, then followed a ten-year detour into chemical engineering before taking up writing again. She is a published, award-winning poet and prose writer. An agent is shopping her first novel, a science and political thriller, to various publishers. Also in the works is a non-fiction book-length work on sex addiction.

M. GARRETT BAUMAN

The Point of Spring

John Joseph Enneking. *Spring Hillside*. Oil on canvas. Museum of Fine Arts, Boston. Gift of the heirs of George Adams Kettell, 1913..

IT'S EARLY MARCH, and crunchy, melted and re-frozen snow persists under four inches of fresh, wet snow. But spring is turning to western New York. Pigeon-toed possum tracks first appeared yesterday, and last night, the possum's white, rat face startled me in the barn. It leaned away in post-hibernation stupor, too groggy to hiss. This morning a cardinal answered my whistle for the first time since last year. A broken maple branch drips sugar sap. The earth flows, stretches dumbly under the icy crust. There would be sun if the warm air had not fogged thickly over the snow. Later, a Canadian front blows in and drops snow through the fog. We're balanced on the dividing point of seasons.

So we're still mindful of winter mistakes and madness. Like the 30 gallon steel drum I neglected to empty of rain water. Expanding ice unrolled the heavy steel seams and blew out its bottom. A car allowed to sink a few inches in wet lawn last November was frozen to earth for weeks. The engine stalled trying to break the wheels loose, and hot water thrown on them froze instead of thawing the ground. Winter is no time for mistakes.

Or bad luck. Our neighbor, who shares a three-quarter-mile gravel right-of-way to our homes on the hill, had carpal tunnel syndrome caused by his factory job. The surgeons cut the warped bones and tendons in John's wrists, then re-attached them. On half pay, alone except for us and his girlfriend on weekends, John felt frozen in. His sixteen-year-old dog, Joey, half-blind and hunchbacked, stopped eating. Medicine failed. John crawled into the dog house and curled around Joey, then realized what was required. "He knew it was coming," John said. "He didn't care. He wanted me to do it." Firing the gun redamaged one wrist. But John appeared at our door dragging the dog's body in a black plastic bag. "Ground's too frozen to dig a hole," he said. "Can I overwinter Joey in your goose house?"

So we lugged the body there. A few days afterward, the bag was gone. I followed boot tracks and the bag's flat trail. They meandered a mile in the woods. John told me later he left Joey under a pine tree with a few boughs over him. "There's a lot of hungry fox and bobcat now," he said. "Joey'll be gone in a week."

The goose house was empty because our goose went winter mad—insisting on swimming in our freezing pond. She paddled hard to keep a few square feet of water melted. To get out, she scrambled against the razor ice edge until blood stained her white feathers. We shooed her—hissing with resentment—to a pen for the winter.

We're all penned in. By cold, over-used bodies, death, and our own shortcomings and mad ideas. We need spring to free us. The creek roars when freed of its icy stupor, raking off the ravine's debris and barriers. It drags away 30-foot logs, this milquetoast, four-inch deep summer creek. If you took a July hike up its waterfalls, you would never suspect the spring violence that scrubs it clean.

Today, chipmunks race across the snow. Freed from hibernation, the males are as spring mad as the creek. The annual descent of their testicles urges them to mate and abandon their usual grouchy solitude. They're not the sociable fellows of cartoons, but nut-snatching misers who spend much of the summer underground guarding their treasures—a kind of waking hibernation. Now they rattle along the gutters like carbonated peppercorns.

Later, two foxes leap up the huge dead oak in the hedgerow. They chase each other like furry snakes twining around the trunk, then stop, sniff the air and gaze at the quiet fields. What simple joy! A pause for love of life on that still point before spring exerts *its* compulsions.

I'm with the foxes, the world all before me, but I know that the season's giant, slow wheel even now turns toward ice again. The earth's angle of incidence to the sun flicks hormones on and off. We are as helpless before May's sunburst of energy as we are before the gloom of the winter solstice. For the fox and chipmunk, it is a seamless circle. They do not know, as I do, that we are allotted only so many trips around.

I take our old yellow tomcat for a walk. He hasn't been out of the house for weeks. His back's bald patches shiver when it's below twenty degrees. When he spots squirrels at the bird feeder, he crouches but no longer springs. So they continue eating under his whiskers. I scatter them for him, and he seems dimly satisfied. As we amble around the house, he pauses, sniffs and blinks, waiting for me to return. I coax him to complete the circle, but he is thinking about the blanket by the sunny window, and we go back the way we came.

Still, it's nearly spring. And spring madness is an abundance of abundance. Now there are a few snow mosquitos; soon no-see-ums will hum in clouds. Thousands of bass fry will flash in the pond. Yellow trefoil and grasshoppers will glut the field, and wood paths will be lit by mists of bluets, gaywings, trillium and dogwood. Creek pools will teem with red-striped chub that nibble toes. What do they do during March's torrents? No fingers to clutch crevices when the mad water thunders and froths overhead.

When spring is a miracle so lovely and we have survived such rage, how can it grow stale? Yet by August, we stare at the abundance as if we are sated. Like the chipmunks, I will sit on my gathered treasure instead of seeking every speck of beauty and life. One tattered bluet whipped by November sleet will make me wish I had stared longer at the thousands. Spring counts most when it isn't spring.

We need to believe energy will spring inside us again, need to hang onto unreasonable hope that somehow comes true each year. Young lovers do not understand why their love cannot expand forever until the universe is filled with bluets. In spring I don't know why myself. For a little while, we are aware that we too are drops of the earth's sap, rising and falling with its tides. For a little while in spring, darkness yields to light, cold to warmth, the inanimate to motion. And then the wheel turns. On the point of spring you balance knowing this and blissfully forgetting.

M. GARRETT BAUMAN is the author of two books and fiction and essays in many journals. This essay was supported by a generous grant from the Constance Saltonstall Foundation in Ithaca, New York.

ELISA LEIGH

This November Day

How much brush was left for you to cut, George, the sun just beginning
to melt away last night's dark, your breath fogging the one-man camper.
It was time to put the giving soil to bed, and you were ready for work,
old man's hands chilled with morning's grip, face lined as a palm.
Stepping out into the day, November wind catching your hair the way you
were in the brush hog's chains. The machine finally brought you to rest,
no danger of tidying up. The last acres were still open for business
the way some piece of land always is, when it is Vermont and their land.

You would hitch up hog to tractor, saw in tow, setting out to clear
the boss's land another time, before the last hard freeze took all chance
of cutting till day's end. The hog got you George, down off the tractor's
worn seat, so clearly your shape they'd have to burn it to take you
completely away. Caught in the hog's jaws, dragged from your early work,
you were blooming carmine when everything around was tawny.

How much brush was taken before the machine took you, turning against
the hand that made it run, chewing the life out as it was built to do, strong
chains against your farm hand's flesh. The field that yielded to your tractor's
pull these twenty years, took without consent, one last soaking drink
of your working man's blood. This November day we are asked to accept
that this temporary condition we recognize as living is as willing to leave us
brush hogged and bleeding as the godforsaken machine that took your life.

Elisa Leigh

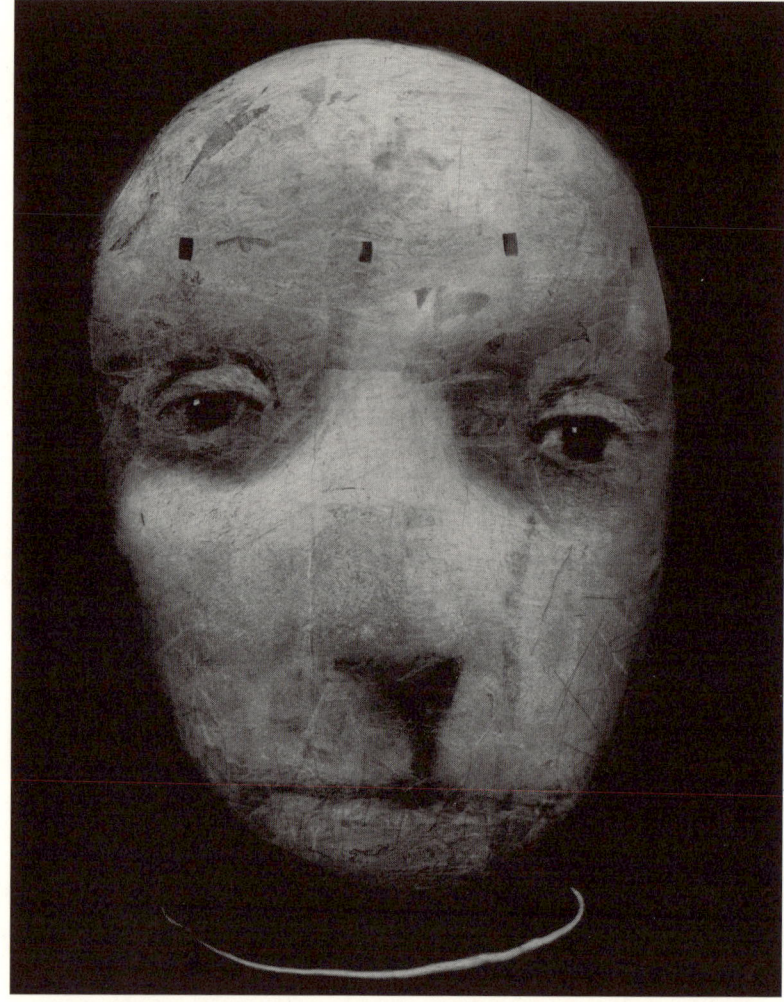

Alan Magee.
Memoir.
©1990, Alan
Magee, monotype
14×11 in.

This November day you could not finish the job you started,
full intending to ride tractor back to barn, hop down and be done,
like so many days before. Those working days your life
was indecipherable from the work you gave in daily doses,
never questioning if the brush that remained was substantial
enough to throw your life in front of it, one man at a time.

ELISA LEIGH has an bachelor's degree in creative writing from Sarah Lawrence College and, from the School for International Training, a degree in English as a Second Language . ALAN MAGEE's monotype, *Memoir,* is part of a one-person exhibition at the Berlin Philharmonic Hall, November 6–27, 2000. A forty-page catalog, *Archive, Alan Magee Monotypes,* featuring twenty-two related works, as well as *Archive,* a limited edition, boxed suite of six giclée prints will be available from www.darkwoodpress.com or from www.alanmagee.com.

PART IV

Coming of Age

MICHAEL NETHERCOTT

The Harvesters

IT IS THE BEGINNING OF MUCH—one man's earliest full memory. True, there are prior images: the confinement of a crib, a certain birthday cake, a bathtub overflowing . . . but these are only visual flashes, lacking any real sense of narrative. This memory, however, is sufficiently detailed as to provide a story. In it, he is perhaps five years old.

Late autumn. A meadow. A pack of children (he the youngest). The meadow is where it starts, this chain of remembrance. They make a circle of seven or eight kids, his cousins and their neighbors. Their eyes are plunged into the magical, awful thing-in-the grass. A girl cousin—Agnes, is it?—wants it to be only part of a stuffed toy. An older neighbor boy scoffs away that comfort. The thing-in-the grass is nothing less than a hoof, severed unfathomably from some creature of the wilds. The consensus comes around to a deer. Yes, it must be. Someone demands, "Where's the rest gone?" It is a disturbing contemplation.

Next, the woods. Shedding off warmth and light, the tribe moves through relentless tree shadows. This is a place unsanctioned by parents. He hurries to keep pace with the longer legs. Then . . .

The pumpkin patch. The kids stand among the odd, overblown fruit. A Halloween crop, appearing like ghosts in the heart of a great journey. Some fragile sorcery is at play here. How else to explain this sudden country of abundance? Armies of pumpkins. A low galaxy of them. They rest in memory as limitless, stretching ever onward toward soulful horizons. They are almost painfully gorgeous in their multiplicity. Particularly when you are so small and finite and have been squeezed out of the protective skin of home and parents.

This placid kingdom is now under siege. One of the boys has ripped a fruit from its vine and hurled it through air. It strikes down, bursting on a rock. Another child mirrors the action, then another,

Opposite:
Thomas Sully.
The Torn Hat.
Oil on panel, 1820.
Museum of Fine Arts,
Boston. Gift of
Miss Belle Greene and
Henry Copley Greene in
memory of their mother,
Mary Abby Greene
(Mrs. J.S. Copley
Greene), 1916.
Photograph ©2000,
Museum of Fine Arts,
Boston.

and another. Some pumpkins fly apart; some are dented and scarred. They all smack loudly as they land. It is the sound of irreparability.

There has been no planning of this, no discussion. And now, as more of the band join in, not a word disturbs the purity of action. It is as if some unseen whisperer had issued a command. In moments, all save one have committed themselves to the work.

The rememberer alone stands off, watching the scene with amazement and apprehension. It is such a strange pageant—sloweddown and deliberate, unaccompanied by apparent emotion. Neither anger nor excitement, glee nor frenzy, propels the activity. Pumpkin after pumpkin detonates in swift succession. How many? Must it be all? Will they seize every one, from here to the setting sun?

The rememberer finally bends through time to press his hands to one small orange sphere. Smooth and cool to the touch, it requires him. Is he not one of this band? Though the youngest and most distant-born, he is pledged to his companions by his very presence here. Their dismays and glories are his to taste. A few grunting tugs, and it comes loose. He lifts his prey high and, with all the strength he has been given, throws it. The pumpkin swings through low clouds, plummets, and dies magnificently with the sound of deadened thunder.

This is completion. This is finality. Neither surgery nor alchemy can restore what has been broken here. He does not know how to feel.

Then a voice, booming and hoarse with rage. It scatters the slayers of the crop, and all but the rememberer flee into the forest. He is left alone then, held to the earth by phantom vines of fear and awe. His eyes are as full as haunted moons. The farmer, a giant of anger, is quickly upon him, cursing, hollering, invoking vicious threats of parents and police. He who has lived the fewest years will be sacrificed for the sins of his breed.

But now, directly between his smallness and the enormity of retaliation, there steps a figure of calm and deliverance. It is one of the older boys who has left safety to come shield him. This one now speaks directly to the farmer, with unflinching eyes, offering guileless apology and strong oaths of reparation. The wronged man's wrath slowly abates. The small boy has not swallowed all his protector's words; he only knows that some bargain has been struck which may yet spare him. The farmer nods to himself and, turning sharply, beckons the older boy to follow. The two of them shrink forever away across the field.

The rememberer stands and watches, holding down tremulous sobs. A summons from the woods turns his head. Agnes and others are ordering him to run. Freed from that place of admonishment, the small boy hurries to his companions, and they all, the graced survivors, race madly through the wilderness. Precious miles are wedged between the murdered harvest and safe haven. Then… Parents. Withheld truths. Departures.

The aftermath becomes gray and untenable in memory. What does stand forth in the tumble of recollections is the fact that the boy who shielded him would, several years later, perish in some unpronounceable corner of a war. For the rememberer, this reality has somehow fallen back to blend with—and to heighten—the sacrifice in the pumpkin patch.

The older boy, though neither friend nor blood relation, rose up as The One Who Profoundly Returns, the one who will not abandon you to the dark and lonely fate that you have purchased for yourself. The older boy offered his own guilty spirit in exchange for the younger's future awareness. He would not leave a comrade behind.

And this is what remains for the man who was the smallest boy: there is terror, indeed, in the wild realms of experience, but also there is true compassion. And the opportunity to purge the heart of its shame.

MICHAEL NETHERCOTT's stories, poems and sketches have appeared in various national periodicals including *The Magazine of Fantasy and Science Fiction*, *Cobblestone*, and *Plays, the Drama Magazine for Young People*. He is a performer and organizer of theater events, and makes his home in the rural enclave of Guilford, Vermont, with his wife, daughter and son.

JAMES WARD

Forged and Tempered
Raymond Comes of Age

IN AUGUST 1969, Raymond Weaver would have said he was a man: graduated from high school, gone to work in the mill, registered for the draft, almost nineteen.

He lived with his mother in a small frame house on the city's industrial South Side. Summer evenings they would sit on their front porch in weatherworn green and white plastic lawn chairs, his mother crocheting and watching the children playing ball in the middle of Keppel Street, Raymond looking over the roofs of Keppel's tightly packed houses and through the metal branches of their television antennas, his gaze fixed on the flame from the steel mill's tallest smokestack and the patch of sky it lit to a purplish pink. Sometimes they would eat supper on the porch and sit there until long after dark, but if the mill's fumes drifted their way they would retreat inside to escape the heavy, sulfurous smell, as if it had just rained rotten eggs.

Friday evenings, at eight-thirty, Raymond would put on a clean tee-shirt and yank a brush through his short, curly hair. Before leaving the house he would check the television listings hoping he could find a movie his mother would enjoy (she liked detective stories). After he said goodnight to her, he would walk two blocks to Kepple Street's dead-end and Murphy's Tavern. He was thirty years younger than Murphy's regulars, but he liked being with them. And he knew they liked him, because he had overheard them saying so.

"Good kid, that Raymond."
"Working in the mill, ain't he?"

"Yeah. The finishing mill."

"His mother did a good job with him."

"Polite kid. Respectful."

"What was he when his old man left? Was he five yet?"

"I dunno."

"Yeah. Must've been about five."

Raymond's mother never spoke about that, and he never asked about it, whether he was four or five or six. It didn't make any difference.

It was Friday and a cool night for August. The regulars were in Murphy's. Raymond sat down on a vinyl-topped stool at the far end of the bar. He remembered when he was a boy and the guys at the bar would call him in off the street to give him buffalo-head nickels. Murphy's barroom hadn't changed since then—the size of an ordinary living room, with a mahogany bar that ran its full length, its middle marked by taps for three draft beers—Budweiser, Simon Pure and Iroquois. Behind the bar were shelves of whiskey bottles, a plate glass mirror, and a television. The same juke box still sat against the wall and the same small pool table was in the middle of the room, parallel to the bar. A door at the back still led to the small partitioned bathroom. Raymond liked the constancy of Murphy's—permanent as steel.

Stan and Lenny sat along the middle of the bar with their feet propped on the bottom rungs of their stools. Three old timers sat quietly at the other end where they always sat drinking shots of whiskey with beer chasers. Stan and Lenny were about fifty, and both wore white, short sleeved T-shirts. Stan's shirt stretched over his stomach, as tight as a tourniquet. Lenny was short with a thick neck and thick arms. He reminded Raymond of a fireplug with a crew cut.

Stan looked out the front window. Except for dim halos, Kepple Street's lampposts had vanished in a leaden fog that closed Murphy's off from the world. Raymond bet himself that Stan had seen worse and would say so.

He had. And he did. "I always said the worst fog I ever seen was in London in the war. I always said that. I always said the worst fog I ever seen was on Blackfriar's bridge. I always said that."

Lenny swirled the beer at the bottom of his glass, first one direction, then the other. He drank up and pushed his empty to the edge of the bar.

Stan started, "I always said . . ."

Lenny interrupted, "I always said you was full of it."

Raymond enjoyed the arguments in Murphy's, and they were almost as common as the lying.

At about ten o'clock Raymond noticed the steady hum of the beer cooler's electric motor. He looked up to see why the bar was so quiet. Two kids had walked in, skinny things, with hair to their shoulders. They smiled at the bartender. He didn't smile back.

Raymond wondered how these two had found Murphy's—it had neither a sign on its front nor neon beer ads in its windows. A single-story clapboard building stained dingy gray from accumulated pollution, it could have been somebody's garage or storage shed. The tavern didn't need advertising. Murphy's was for the men of Kepple Street.

These two kids weren't from Kepple Street. One wore bell-bottom pants and multicolored shoes—red, white and blue; the other, jeans, sneakers, and a faded army coat, its sleeves decorated with military patches. They took two stools near Raymond. The bartender scrutinized their proof and reluctantly poured them drafts—short ones, fifteen cents each. They said, "Thanks."

The kid in the army coat picked up a quarter from his bar change and slotted it into the pool table. The balls dropped with a loud, clanking chorus. A shaded bulb hung over the table. The kid pulled its thin chain. The table's green felt lit up, like an exhibit's centerpiece. He took a pool cue from the wall rack and looked down its length as though sighting a rifle. Satisfied it was straight, he took a little square of blue chalk from the table's side and coated the cue's tip.

It took only a few minutes before Raymond knew neither one could shoot. And they weren't used to Murphy's narrow dimensions. The only unobstructed shots were from the table's ends—side shots meant interference, from the window or the barstools. The wall rack held a cut-off stick for the side shots, but they didn't notice it. Raymond considered telling them about it. He didn't. No one else did.

"They shoot like sissies."

It came from the other end of the bar, loud enough for everyone to hear and loud enough for Raymond to recognize Lenny's voice. Lenny had been at the bar that morning when Raymond walked to work. Raymond knew what that meant. Lenny was on vacation. After twenty-five years the mill gave him three weeks each year. He spent them at Murphy's. If his wife called, whoever answered the phone would look around, smile, and ask if there was anyone in the joint named Lenny. Once, she came to get him. The next day Lenny said he had, "Beat the old lady and slept with the dog." She never came again. But Lenny was the most regular of all.

"You know, it ain't right."

"Forget it Lenny," Stan said.

Lenny shook his head. "A young punk like him? He's got no right to wear that coat."

Stan looked up at the clock and said to the bartender, "The news is coming on." Then he bought Lenny another beer and aimed him at the television.

Lenny stood up and said he had to "Drain the monster." On his route to the bathroom he stared at the two kids. Raymond knew Lenny was hoping they would stare back. They didn't.

Lenny stopped and clapped Raymond on the knee. "How you doin' Raymond?"

"Fine, Lenny."

"Yeah? You still going to that college?"

"Two nights a week."

"That's good. But you watch what they tell you there." Lenny walked to the bathroom.

Lately, Raymond's thoughts about Lenny had been banging into one another. There was the way Lenny could push steel, day after day, year after year, in the heat and dust—none of Raymond's professors could hack that, not for an hour; and the way Lenny was so sure about everything (I made a mistake *once*—I thought I was wrong about something, but I wasn't). Raymond wished he could be as sure of anything as Lenny was of everything. But then there was the way Lenny dismissed everything outside his narrow world—if he didn't know it or like it, it wasn't worth knowing or liking.

Lenny made it back to the bar in time for the eleven o'clock news: the day's top stories for August 22, 1969—with commentary from Murphy's:

Antiwar activists vowed to keep protesting until the war stops. Thousands marched up Sixth Avenue in New York.

"Look at 'em."

"They look like bums."

"A good boot in the backside is what they need."

Raymond checked his mail each evening, expecting his draft notice. He didn't dread it, didn't desire it. Just expected it. His mother wanted him to go to college full time, get a deferment and earn a degree. She said that she could earn what was necessary to get by, and he could earn what was necessary to get ahead.

That wasn't what Raymond day-dreamed about. He fantasized about returning to Murphy's after decorated war service, how they would greet him, and the special place he would have there. He had already thought out how he would handle his heroism—he would be quiet about it, not wear it out like Stan did his.

California investigators continued their search for the killer of actress Sharon Tate, who was found murdered in her Beverly Hills home. The killers left a calling card, the word "pig" smeared in blood on a door.

"I wish they'd break in here, on Keppel."

"Why the hell would they break in on Keppel? You think they think we got movie stars here?"

"Maybe they'll break in your joint. Maybe they think your old lady's a movie star."

"Damn. They broke in my joint . . . wake up my old lady in the middle of the night . . . I'd like to see 'em try that."

"If they broke in and saw your old lady in the middle of the night, they'd be so ascared they'd all pass out."

A massive gathering of young people, estimated at close to 400,000, survived endless traffic jams, food and water shortages, and torrential downpours to proclaim the Woodstock Festival a fantastic success.

"Look at 'em."

"Look at that one."

"They got a baby with them."

"Animals. They're just animals."

Consensus never lasted long in Murphy's. Soon another argument had started, and Stan raised his voice to Lenny, "You ever seen combat?"

Lenny waived his hand in dismissal. "Don't pull that on me, Stanley."

"You ever seen combat Lenny? I'm asking you that. A simple question."

"Yeah. I seen combat."

"You did? You seen combat?"

"Yeah. I seen combat."

A disbelieving, "Where'd you see combat Lenny?"

"Right down here, on Kepple Street—that's where I seen combat."

The two kids continued to shoot pool and nurse their beers. The one in the Army coat walked to the juke box and looked through its glass cover. The bartender said, "No music. We're watching the television." The kid stepped away from the juke box and took his turn at the pool table. He tried to bank the eight ball, missed badly and laughed. He surrendered the pool cue to his friend and went back to his seat.

Lenny stood up and walked alongside the bar. Raymond thought it was an unannounced trip to the bathroom, but Lenny stopped in front of the kid. The kid took a drink of his beer and started to turn toward the pool table. He never made it around. Lenny swung his right arm, launching it from near Murphy's floor, and slapped the kid hard on the side of the head. Raymond jumped and spilled his beer over the bar.

Lenny snatched at the collar of the kid's army coat and yanked it down. Then he grabbed it with both hands and pulled harder. The coat came off. Lenny said, "You ain't wearin' that in here."

The kid started to say something. Lenny hit him again, with an open hand, right on the ear. It made a sharp sound, like someone flopping flat into a pool of water. The kid covered his face and fell back against the bar.

Lenny threw the coat on the floor, at the bottom of the barstool, and walked back to his seat. "That coward there . . . he ain't gonna wear that in this place."

The kid made a sniffling sound. Raymond's leg shook, and his throat was dry. He looked at the kid's friend, who stood on the far side of the pool table, as still as if he had turned to stone. The bartender took a towel and soaked up Raymond's beer, then refilled his glass.

Raymond looked down at the Army coat, then leaned over and asked the kid, "You okay?"

"I'm dizzy. I don't feel good." He was having trouble sitting straight.

Raymond picked the coat off the floor and put it in the kid's lap. Lenny walked toward the kid again. He stopped in front of him and the kid cowered. Lenny looked at the coat and asked, "Where'd you get that?"

"It's my father's. He gave it to me."

Lenny pointed his finger at the coat. "You respect that."

Raymond watched Lenny walk to the bathroom. He walked deliberately—plodding to hide his drunkenness while swaggering to display his manliness. The kid's friend helped him off the stool and out the front door.

The television made the only sound in the room until the bartender spoke. "Looks like I lost a customer, huh?"

Laughter and, "You don't think he'll be coming back soon?"

"To be slapped like that—and just sit there."

"Slapped in the face."

"His friend didn't do nothing either."

"Slapped like that."

"I'd rather be punched than that."

Lenny came back to the bar. He glanced at the two empty stools, then told the bartender, "Give everyone a drink and one for yourself."

Stan drank up and the bartender poured him a refill. Raymond still had a full glass of beer. The bartender said, "Drink up. You got one coming on Lenny."

Raymond picked up his beer. He stared at it and set it back down. He got off his stool and started toward the front door.

"Hey, where you going? Lenny wants to buy you one."

Raymond didn't look back at the bartender, or at Lenny. He said, "No. I think it's time I got out of here."

"I'll hold one for you."

Raymond said, "Don't bother."

JAMES WARD is currently working on his first collection of short stories. He lives in Morristown, New Jersey, with his wife, Barbara.

Edward Hopper. *Night Shadows*. Etching, 6⅞ × 8¼, 1921. Sheldon Memorial Art Gallery, University of Nebraska–Lincoln F.M. Hall Collection.

Pageant

The youngest girls sob when hair spray
burns in their eyes because they need
poofy hair. The woman hairdresser
comforts them with stories of kittens,
Lassie-type dogs who rescue children
exposed on the hillsides, or she mentions
pizza and cheeseburgers. They wait
their turn on stage where they will dance,
juggle flowers, their minty-breath words
spoken loud so that everyone can hear
how they will make it to the eighth grade,
excel in math, teach their dogs new tricks;
a world opens with possibility, but for now
their mascara has run. The mothers,
ex-beauty queens themselves, chew
on their cuticles, waiting in the wings
for their little darlings to belt out a song,
tap dance their moment of greatness.
This is middle America, little girls strut
their potential. Way up high on the stage
rafters, a sand bag is about to break off
and fall on the center of the stage, missing
contestant #7, barely, and she continues
to act the scene from Romeo and Juliet
lost in a cloud of dust, putting out a hand,
saying, "O Romeo," and the SNEEZE!
The girl's mother wants to faint, does,
and falls back on the lap of a grandfather
who can hardly keep back the tears.
Who could resist them, these darling girls
on the verge of how the world waits for them?

VIRGIL SUAREZ was born in Havana, Cuba, but has lived in the United States since 1974. He is the author of over a dozen books of prose and poetry. Currently he is working on a new collection of poems titled *Gusano*. He divides his time between Miami and Tallahassee.

ROBERTA BOLDUC

Spiritual Eldering

Frank Blackwell Mayer. *Independence (Squire Jack Porter)*. Oil on paperboard, 1858. Smithsonian American Art Museum, Harriet Lane Johnston Collection.

THE WOMAN IN THE CHAIR ACROSS FROM ME was not your typical nursing home resident. Aside from the three-pronged walker standing ready to assist her, she looked normal—normal being the antithesis of ghostlike souls with fixed stares who roamed the hallways of the nursing homes where I have visited in my work. Her well-groomed appearance and alert manner caught me off guard.

After exchanging pleasantries she confided she had resided there for some time. Often residents, ashamed to admit to the stigma of dependency, would wistfully explain their residence there was "temporary." But she added grimly "And I hate every minute of it."

I searched for a glimmer of hope. "What about the activities here?" I asked. "Surely there must be something enjoyable, some hobby or interest that could be pursued."

She turned her eyes away. "Well, there's always Bingo."

Long after her name left my conscious mind, the defeated look in her eyes stayed with me. Why do we warehouse our elders? What indelible change in our society caused us to demote elders from a place of wisdom and honor in our collective lives?

Up until the Industrial Revolution elders were woven into the fabric of social life. The marks of age and experience were displayed as a badge of honor with no attempt at camouflage. It was elders who transmitted the great myths, rituals, and special knowledge needed for culture to continue from one generation to the next.

The elder's place of honor in the family was lost as young men migrated to the cities to find work in newly built factories. Traditional knowledge formerly passed from father to son and mother to daughter grew obsolete as schools and professional organizations took on the role of teachers. Absolved of any productive role in the community or family structure, elders became disempowered as society's view of them slowly shifted from respect to ambivalence.

We now live in a culture where old age is synonymous with uselessness. When adults reach the age of sixty-five, they are "retired" from the community and workforce. Our fear of aging causes us to segregate elders into "retirement" homes where they are a less visible reminder of our own aging. Physical frailty and loss of independence consign oldsters to nursing homes where widespread abuses underscore the contempt assigned to old age. Beyond the insult to this still vibrant and valuable segment of our populace is the untold damage done to ourselves and our children as we are deprived of mentors and role models for living.

In our fast-paced, money-driven society wisdom is a commodity both unappreciated and in short supply. We live on a planet under siege as we stagger from one world-threatening crisis to the next, devoid of mentors.

A CHANGE IS ON THE HORIZON. Over the next few decades our definition and attitude toward aging will undergo a radical transformation. In ten years one-third of the U.S. population will be over fifty. As baby boomers have redefined every life stage encountered over the past fifty years, they will next revolutionize old age.

In some nursing homes, the breakthrough has already begun. The Eden Alternative, a more natural, holistic approach to long-term care, is transforming them. Instead of closeting people where they go to die, these nursing homes are becoming "habitats where individuals go to continue to grow and enjoy life." The brainchild of Dr. William Thomas, this approach incorporates introducing live-in pets, daily activities with children, and live plants and gardens for residents to care for and harvest. The sterile, institutional setting is exchanged for a diverse, stimulating environment where residents are given the emotionally nourishing opportunity to give care to other living things. Staff empowerment, a key component of the program, results in empowering of the resident. The intergenerational element, often experienced through on-site daycare centers that benefit the staff and the community, provides a dual advantage. Residents, no longer segregated from other age groups, fulfill a need to be useful and needed, and children in need of elder role models receive valuable lessons in life.

In all probability the need for nursing home care will come later in life as people live longer and healthier lives into their seventies, eighties, and nineties and, given the awesome breakthroughs in medical technology and genetics, perhaps beyond. Will this simply mean a longer work life or an interminable quest for the fountain of youth? Rabbi Zalman Schachter-Shalomi, founder of the Spiritual Eldering Institute in Philadelphia, believes there are more crucial roles for future elders to assume. The sane, sensible, and wise stewardship of our human resources and planet, says Reb Zalman, will result in a long needed resumption of the ancient role of elders in our society.

For seniors to be up to this paramount task, they must embrace the reality of aging and all the promise it holds, rather than fearfully retreating from it. Reb Zalman, author of *From Age-ing to Sage-ing* and student of Sufi and Buddhist teachers, consciousness researchers, and humanistic and transpersonal psychologists, teaches people to harvest the wisdom they have acquired over a lifetime. At seventy-two, Reb Zalman maintains that our senior years offer greater opportunity for self-knowledge and inner growth than any other stage in life. At his workshops and seminars, people are taught to use meditation, relaxation techniques, and breathing exercises to awaken intuitive abilities. Their relationship with God and the cosmos is explored, and they are invited to own up to very human failings, repair important personal relationships, and reflect on their life experiences. They are brought to the realization that their struggle for meaning and value in life has been worthwhile, and that even the failures and fiascos have eventually led to unexpected successes.

This is, however, more than a self-serving exercise for the attendees. The end result, from Reb Zalman's viewpoint, is to revive the tradition of tribal elders, "sages who will feed wisdom back into society and who will guide the long-term reclamation project of healing our beleagured planet. Once elders are restored to positions of leadership, they will function as wisdomkeepers, inspiring us to live by higher values that will help convert our throwaway lifestyle and by serving as evolutionary pathfinders offering hope and guidance to those searching for models of a fulfilled human potential."

As the Spiritual Eldering concept becomes more widespread, Sage-ing Centers are sprouting across the country. Reb Zalman predicts these centers will replace today's senior centers. Sage-ing centers train and support elders in Spiritual Eldering techniques and offer life affirming support and encouragement. They will also serve to educate communities on the vital need of, once again, having elders assume a prominent role in our culture.

ROBERTA BOLDUC is a freelance writer in Charlotte, North Carolina. She hopes to impart her spiritual eldering beliefs to her two granddaughters, Emily Ruth and Sarah Rose.

EDWARD DEREGIBUS

First Flight

Missy DeRegibus. *First Flight.* Pencil, 2000.

EDDIE REGARDED THE STREET FROM HIS VANTAGE POINT beneath the Elm tree; he made a quick calculation and dashed across, turning his ankles to run along the outer rims of his soles before coming to rest on a lonely island of crunchy, straw-colored grass. The summer sun had turned the asphalt street into a superheated misery for bare feet. Heavy American cars lumbered over the black tar making it sticky to his feet. Traces of tar would still be there when he started school in another month. School. His mind carefully avoided the subject without even knowing it and settled on more pressing matters, such as where the next shady spot was in his route to Dan Allen's house halfway up the block.

Dan was only a year younger than he and had been his closest friend ever since moving to east 13th street. Dan was solid, an only child of older parents who were very careful about evil in the world. In the early 1950s you had to look harder to find evil, but it was there, usually sporting long sideburns. Eddie was the taller of the two and both had skinny, sunburnt bodies. Summers, Ed was so dark that his Uncle Shi had taken to calling him Indian, pronounced "engine." Saturdays they would go to the movies and then play whatever it was they had seen when they got home. Many a trade would involve dialogue like; "Ok, I'll trade you my space men for your old cap pistol if we'll play cowboys after the movie."

Today, summer had really hit its stride and the sun beat down on him as he made his zig-zag journey up the street. It had been so long since there had been any rain that the mesquite bushes and scrub grass had given up their hold on the fine sand which now spilled over the curb from the vacant lot across the street. The cool, pleasant light of morning had changed after lunch to a fiery, yellow world. The wind had steadily picked up, and the sand was beginning to blow. With the sandstorms they had been having lately an idea had steadily grown that just might work. That was the problem. He always had lots of ideas but didn't seem to be able to get them to work. There had been the submarine idea, inspired by the Civil War prototype. It had seemed simple enough, all he needed was a barrel made waterproof with tar, a long snorkle, and a simple hand crank to provide some manner of directional propulsion. Yet, after many drawings and much planning it remained a bunch of old boards crudely nailed together with used, rusty nails and imagination.

Sometimes he played that it would work, but the fact was it didn't work and probably never would. Still, this new idea was different, and for once he had all the necessary stuff.

Mrs. Allen answered the door in her slow, quiet manner. "No, Daniel isn't home, he has gone with his father to work at his grandparent's farm today, but I'll tell him you called." She left the screen door and retreated to the darkened bedroom and the fan. Ed waited on the shady porch, resting his scorched feet on the wonderfully cool concrete. Well, no matter, he was still going to try it, even if no one was there to see it. Running home using the bleached out yards where he could, he hurried along. The wind was picking up and he still had a few things to get ready.

The air-conditioned air in the house hit him full in the face, drying the sweat on his forehead instantly. Carefully he closed the door to his room. He didn't want anyone asking questions; they might not approve. Rummaging through the closet and his old toy chest, he threw things in a pile, then found the nearly new beach towel in the bottom of his chest of drawers. It had been given to him on his last birthday by a well-meaning but overly practical relative. After putting on his shoes, he carefully tied the two top corners of the towel to his wrists and the two bottom corners to his waist, took his roller skates in one hand and his snorkeling mask in the other, and went out the door. The sandstorm had arrived, the sky was a reddish brown, and the blowing sand stung his bare legs. Leaning into the wind with head down he walked to the top of the block. No one was out, the younger kids were all taking naps, and the rest were probably playing in their rooms or watching TV.

At the top of the block he sat down on the curb to put on his skates and adjust the mask. He stood sideways for a moment testing the strength of the wind; his Dad wouldn't be doing flying lessons today. After checking up the street for cars, he skated to the middle of the street where the asphalt was worn smooth and with a dramatic flourish spread his arms wide. The beach towel sailed out with a snap; only by quickly bending his knees did he avoid falling. This was working better than expected—the sail strained against his arms and back, cutting into his wrists. After fixing one of the corners of the towel that didn't hold, he continued to pick up speed as gravity and the wind hurried him on.

Boy, this was keen! The skates roared as they passed over rough patches in the street. He felt elated. Where was everyone, anyway? Once he almost fell when he hit a sand drift and suddenly decelerated. He would have avoided it, but the mask had fogged over as perspiration poured down his face. He righted himself and steered back into the middle of the street; fortunately no cars had yet appeared. He was moving along at a good clip now, but the end of the block was coming up where the city-maintained street abruptly ended in a sand-chocked dirt road. Making a quick decision, he decided to plow into the foot-deep sand drifts and see how far he could get.

The answer came quickly as the skates halted about eight inches into the drift. He lay on his side facing the street; his collapsed sail half covered him, while the bottoms of his feet tingled like crazy. He wasn't hurt, and it was pleasant to lie there with the wind making that "shushing" sound as it rearranged the deep sand around him. The problem with sandstorms was that they stung your eyes, but with his mask on he could lie there and be completely at ease as long as he kept his mouth shut.

He lay completely motionless enjoying the glory of a successful experiment; the crash landing just added to the fun. Suddenly his neighbor, Mr. Dickson the local sheriff, came out onto his porch and looked across the street where he lay. Eddie raised his top leg, skate and all straight in the air, as a kind of salute. Immediately, Mr. Dickson went back inside without a backward glance. Well, it was probably time to get up and try it again anyway. He got to his feet and tied one of the strings that had come loose in the crash. This was going to be good, he had got the hang of it now.

Boy, he was really going to sail; if only there was somebody around to see it. Still, great inventors didn't allow things like that to get in their way.

ED DEREGIBUS is a native-born west Texan who grew up in a world of tumble weeds, arrowheads, rattlesnakes, and "blue northerns." He has since relocated to the older, more civilized world of Virginia, where he, his wife Missy, and three children reside.

CAROL LEM

Melon Soup
(to Marilyn Chin)

I, too, have come home
spent by the day to watch my mother
hunched over the sink
clean out the pulp of a winter melon.

I do not ask why it is a New Year's treat,
this melon that has lived through holidays,
cured common colds, celebrated birth,
marriages and death; survived family breakups
from East 23rd Street to Madison,
Ah Wing's to Lem's Cafe.

[Artist unknown]. *Proto-Yue Bowl with Incised Lotus Decoration.* White stoneware with gray-green glaze and incised lotus petal design, 6th century. Yale University Art Gallery. Gift of John Hadley Cox, B.A., 1935.

Though weakened by age, she drifts between
bedroom and kitchen.
It takes all night to brew melon soup.

She tells me to turn the flame low,
skim the fat, "Uncle Bill will want something hot
when he brings the chicken in the morning.
Everything for good luck. Wrap these coins
in red paper for your cousins."

I never question the jade and gold
that circle neck, wrist, finger.
Some things you accept without asking.
Short of breath, she takes small steps
to the boiling pot and sips, "less pork."
And gives me another gift.

This unseen talisman
cleans out the seedy mush of a memory
until word by word, tired or not,
I, too, reach my bowl of steaming soup,
blow gently, and drink.

When there is nothing left but the rind
and a daughter's tribute, it is time again
to hunch over the desk and prepare
the winter melon.

CAROL LEM, born and raised in Los Angeles, teaches creative writing and literature at East Los Angeles College. Her poetry has appeared most recently in *Blue Mesa Review, California Quarterly, Cedar Hill Review, Hawaii Pacific Review, Luna,* and *Onthebus.* Carol Lem's books include *Searchings, Grassroots, Don't Ask Why, The Hermit, The Hermit's Journey: Tarot Poems for Meditation,* and *Moe, Remembrance.* Her work is also represented in the anthology *The Geography of Home: California's Poetry of Place.*

PART V

Exuberant Seasons

BEVERLY FLEMING

June, 1941

In the photograph you are in your prime:
body shapely, hair curled back behind
your ears, red tendrils tamed for once.
You wear glasses framed with gold,
the only picture that exists of you
with spectacles, painting you
serious, strong.

As always you are stylish, summer dress
chic in the way of the 'forties, belt enclosing
your slender waist, rayon fabric falling cool
around your perfect legs. You have an air
of sureness standing by the stone wall
bordering the lake, right arm circling
'round the small girl seated next to you.

I am three years old, a shy child
with brown hair pulled into braids
and tied with ribbons. I wear a
flowered sunsuit and white sandals,
gaze uncertain at the camera.

All is well in our lives the year
before Daddy dies, before
the burden of earning a living
and raising two children falls
on your slight frame.

But this is June, 1941, a blue-skied day.
Sunbeams dance behind us on gently

rippling waves of Lake Nipmuc,
named for the tribe that settled
the rocky land, made trails through
field and forest, stopped to cup
their hands and drink the spring-fed
waters, paddled to the center in canoes,
fished for wide-mouth bass
my father deftly catches.

BEVERLY FLEMING is a former psychiatric nurse, who lives with her family and writes, among other things, about her experiences growing up as the daughter of a mother of Irish descent and of a father of French and American Indian descent.

JOHN WREN-LEWIS

Communication Tongued with Fire

My Encounter with T. S. Eliot

Gilbert and George. *Speakers*. Photograph, gelatin silver print, hand-colored, 1983. ©2000 The Cleveland Museum of Art. John L. Severance Fund, 84.170.

I KNEW ELIOT IN THE 1950S when he was the most senior, and I the most junior, council-member of a teaching centre called St. Anne's House in London's Soho. I was amused to read recently that an American critic has likened Eliot's work in the *Four Quartets* to taking over a bombed-out area in the materialistic jungle of twentieth-century Western culture to establish an arena for spiritual reappraisal, for that was what he and a group of others did quite literally in 1943. Hitler's bombs had destroyed the ancient Anglican church of St. Anne but had left the offices and clergy-house standing; the formidable detective-novelist-turned-religious-playwright Dorothy L. Sayers sought Eliot's help in persuading the Bishop of London to open the building as a "centre for Christian discourse" where lectures could be given. At that time I was a science student at London University, and unbeknownst to each other, Eliot and I were fire-wardens in the same "disfigured streets" he described so vividly in the final *Quartet*. I came to St. Anne's only after the war, when I was asked to lecture there on science and religion, and by then Eliot was already a Nobel Laureate, having been awarded the Literature Prize in 1948.

I thought there was something vaguely familiar about the tall, thin, distinguished-looking elderly man who slipped into the back row just as I began lecturing and slipped out again equally unobtrusively as soon as I stopped. This happened every week for about two months. I realized his identity only when a letter arrived from Eliot, in his capacity as a director of the publishing company Faber and Faber, asking if I would like to do a book on the subject. I was, of course, over the moon, but also quite astonished, not out of modesty but because I'd been arguing fiercely against the conservative Christian orthodoxy of Sayers, Eliot, and the other famous council-member at St. Anne's, C.S. Lewis. I'd come from a home where God was the great Fuhrer in the sky who demanded we all knuckle under to our workers' duties in poverty without protest and would strike us down if we didn't, and although I strongly believed that science didn't disprove the idea of God, I saw traditional Christianity as an even worse enemy of the spirit than the atheism or agnosticism of my scientific colleagues. That letter from Eliot was the first hint of what I came to realize later, that these "conservatives" were at heart far less narrow-minded in their orthodoxy than they're usually given credit for, even by some of their greatest admirers.

I would now rank Eliot and Lewis as early "Sages of Aquarius," forerunners of the great upsurge of free spiritual enquiry that began in the 1960s. Ironically, the St. Anne's chairperson, Dorothy Sayers, was probably the most narrowly orthodox of the four, though it was actually she with whom I became a close friend. Eliot and Lewis were open to the fact of spiritual truth in non-Christian religions, and Lewis wrote a book about it. They saw it as part of their work in reawakening awareness and love of the great worldwide pre-Christian mythic traditions, just as the work of Joseph Campbell and Jean Houston have done in the heyday of the Aquarian movement. Lewis ranged from science fiction to children's stories (the well-known *Narnia* books) for this purpose, and Eliot's poetry is full of classical mythic overtones even when dealing with the most modern themes—for example, *Four Quartets* is a cycle of four long poems (called quartets because four voices can be heard in each) constructed around themes of the four ancient mythic elements—air, earth, water, and fire.

These writers were also very aware, in marked contrast to the most orthodox Christianity of their day and ours, that spirituality involves one's awakening awareness to the natural environment—not sentimental or superstitious *beliefs* about the goodness of nature prior to humanity, but actual *consciousness of place.* Eliot, whose most famous early poem used the metaphor of *The Waste Land* to express materialism's dehumanization of life, went on to express his spiritual vision in the *Quartets* by naming each of the poems after a specific place that had been spiritually important to him. He used his poetic art to explore what it was like to know those places with spiritual consciousness.

The real subject of the poems, however, is consciousness itself rather than the places, and that is what makes Eliot our great poet of the spirit. For spirit *is* consciousness—not your consciousness or mine or anyone's, but consciousness-as-such, the dimension of Isness of Conscious Being, whose play of individualized *doing* is the entire dance of events in place and time. Eliot advances this theme in the first Quartet, the poem of air, which was written nearly a decade before the others and named *Burnt Norton,* after a country house burned down by its owner in the eighteenth century in the English Cotswolds, noted for splendid gardens. This Quartet is about the time and the memories that always haunt such gardens for the discerning eye, like the illusion of children's laughter in the rustling of dry leaves in a sunlit drained pool—children who are now long dead:

> Then a cloud passed, and the pool was empty. . . .
> Go, go, go, said the bird: human kind
> Cannot bear very much reality.

And yet there is that other dimension altogether in the very fact of consciousness itself:

> "To be conscious is not to be in time."

This is the meaning of eternity—not everlasting time ("the waste sad time, stretching before and after") but the all-embracing presentness of Conscious Being or Spirit, which continually creates time and space as the matter of its manifestation-in-doing:

> Except for the point, the still point.
> There would be no dance, and there is only the dance.

That is not a metaphysical belief, it is a plain fact of direct experience *whenever there is full consciousness of the actual process of experiencing;* that is, consciousness of consciousness itself, its being, as well as of the things the conscious person *does.*

I can only say, *there* we have been: but I cannot say where,
And I cannot say, how long, for that is to place it in time.

The tragedy of the ordinary human condition, which in one way or another is the main subject of nearly all Eliot's poetry and the central theme of the *Quartets,* is that this dimension of consciousness is absent from most of life because the whole structure of human living focuses on the temporal business of *doing* (which includes thinking, savoring, emoting, judging, and willing, as well as physical action), to the exclusion of actual experiencing, the nontemporal essence of consciousness:

Time past and time future
Allow but a little consciousness.

In that sense, all human cultures of which we have record have been materialistic in practice, long before materialism emerged in explicit philosophies in recent centuries, when sceptics began to challenge the lip service that was given to the *idea* of spirit in religious cultures. And this practical materialism—the concentration of attention on the matter rather than the spirit of living, on doing rather than being, on time rather than eternity—is tragic because it robs life of its only real satisfaction. For most, such satisfaction comes only in occasional flashes:

The moment in the arbour where the rain beat,
The moment in the draughty church at smokefall

But temporal satisfactions, as the Buddha uncompromisingly insisted, must necessarily end in suffering because of their transcience and shallowness, and the practical materialism of human culture only makes matters infinitely worse by encouraging the idea that getting something better means *doing* something more, or something different. Yet what else is there?

Eliot had been a Buddhist in his younger days—there are many Buddhist ideas in *The Waste Land,* even a quotation from Gautama's famous "Fire Sermon"—and he seems to have carried most of the pessimism sometimes associated (I now think wrongly associated) with Buddhism into the Anglican Christianity he embraced in his mature years. His own life perhaps gave him some reason for this, as was recently exposed on the Australian stage in the play *Tom and Viv,* showing how his difficult character might have been held responsible (not least by his own puritan conscience) for his first wife's breakdown into madness. Also, he could see more clearly than many in the 1930s how war was almost certain to engulf Europe again, with only a weary commercial materialism in the democracies to withstand the monstrous totalitarianism of Nazism and Stalinism—a situation where, in the words of Yeats whom Eliot greatly admired,

> ... the best lack all conviction, and the worst
> Are full of passionate intensity

Eliot's conclusion in *Burnt Norton* was that humanity's tragic and dangerous alienation from the eternity-dimension of spirit must be endemic in the very nature of fleshly existence:

> ... the enchainment of past and future
> Woven in the weakness of the changing body

It was on this issue most of all that the youthful and still very naive John Wren-Lewis chose to challenge the now ageing Nobel Laureate, and was actually encouraged to do so by Eliot's own words in the second *Quartet,* the poem of earth (written after war had come), entitled *East Coker* after the village in Somerset where Eliot's ancestors had lived until Andrew Eliot emigrated to the Massachusetts Bay Colony in 1667. The poem retains Eliot's deep pessimism about the world, but also encourages the young not to be too respectful of their elders:

> Had they deceived us,
> Or deceived themselves, the quiet-voiced elders,
> Bequeathing us merely a receipt for deceit?
> The serenity only a deliberate hebetude,
> The wisdom only the knowledge of dead secrets
> Useless in the darkness. . . .
> There is, it seems to us,
> At best, only a limited value
> In the knowledge derived from experience.
> The knowledge imposes a pattern, and falsifies,
> For the pattern is new in every moment

The point I wanted to dispute was summed up in marvellous poetry in the third *Quartet,* the poem of water named after a group of rocks off the New England coast, *The Dry Salvages* (pronounced "Salwages").

> For most of us, there is only the unattended
> Moment, the moment in and out of time,
> The distraction fit, lost in a shaft of sunlight,
> The wild thyme unseen, or the winter lightning,
> Or the waterfall, or music heard so deeply
> That it is not heard
> at all, but you are
> the music
> While the music lasts. These are only hints and guesses,
> Hints followed by guesses; and the rest
> Is prayer, observance, discipline, thought and action.

I was then, as now, immensely moved by the poetry—in fact, I became that verbal music while it lasted—yet I hated what it was say-

Eddie Arning. *Man Fishing from Rocky Coast.* Oil pastel and pencil on laid green paper, 1970. Abby Aldrich Rockefeller Folk Art Museum, Williamsburg, Virginia. Gift of Dr. and Mrs. Alexander Sackton.

ing, for its conclusion seemed suspiciously like a highbrow version of the pie-in-the-sky-when-you-die religion of my childhood, against which I'd rebelled into science. Faced with the choice of giving up physical existence as hopeless or dismissing those special *moments* as mere passing fancies, I took the latter course, and rejected all mysticism as neurotic delusion, choosing instead a very practical Christian humanism aimed at making the world better at providing the "fruition, fulfilment, security or affection" which Eliot despised.

I felt myself thoroughly vindicated in this choice when in 1949 Eliot returned to his earlier role as playwright with *The Cocktail Party,* in which the heroine, whose mystical longing for those special moments forces her to break away from human relationships to become a nun, finds her fulfilment only in death, martyred by savages ("They crucified her, quite near an anthill.") Yet when I met Eliot later in the 1950s, I found none of the harshness toward ordinary life that his verse seemed to show so clearly, and what was more, his next two plays were altogether gentler, softer, more accepting of the possibility that life might after all be good. The last play in particular, *The Elder Statesman,* depicts a Grand Old Man being unmasked publicly for dishonesties and meannesses in his youth, but eventually coming to forgive himself. He blesses his daughter for her forthcoming marriage with no hint that it is doomed to be a mediocre exercise in vanity, as in *The Cocktail Party,* or end in just "dung and death," as do the rustic marriages of *East Coker,* and then he himself dies peacefully under a beech tree with no hint of the "primitive terror" of *The Dry Salvages*. I couldn't help seeing Eliot himself in that character, for by then he'd married his secretary and apparently found the domestic felicity he'd formerly dismissed as impossible, which must have taken no mean act of self-forgiveness for those conscience-tormenting earlier years. At the time I could only attribute this to the mellowing of age, but I now think there may have been a more profound explanation.

Back then, I paid little attention to the fact that he'd had a heart attack from which he nearly died in 1951, just before I had that letter from him; I'm not sure I even knew about it. Today, however, I know from the researches of Dr. Kenneth Ring in America, Dr. Cherie Sutherland here, and many others around the world, as well as from my own personal experience, that coming close to death can, for many people, bring a major mystical opening of consciousness that goes altogether beyond those "hints followed by guesses," which the Eliot of the *Quartets* believed were the best that most of us could expect in this life. It also often brings a profound self-forgiveness. When I was trying to write an account for *Pallicom* in 1985 of my own near-death experience or NDE two years before, I actually found a phrase form *East Coker* running through my head as the perfect description:

I will say to my soul, Be still, and let the dark come upon you,
Which shall be the darkness of God.

It was, I knew, a reference to the mystical writings of St. John of the Cross, but until the NDE I'd taken it to mean simply the prayerful acceptance of life's worst derelictions, perhaps including death itself. In the NDE, however, I encountered a Living Dark which was, quite simply, "eternity in love with the productions of time," an all-embracing love for everything at the very ground of consciousness as such, the "everything" including me and all my weaknesses and nastinesses, past and present. And it has stayed with me day and night ever since, thereby demonstrating that "enchainment" of consciousness to past and future is *not*, definitely not, "woven in the weakness of the changing body." Whatever *is* responsible for the common eternity-blindness of the ordinary human condition, it can be cured this side of the grave for anyone, as I'm sure both the Buddha and Jesus knew—and my suspicion now is that Eliot discovered at least something of this in his heart attack. I think he came back knowing that all those "guesses" at mystical truth, for which he'd struggled to find the right words drawing on the "hints" of special moments and the works of the great mystics, were actually the basic properties of his own *everyday* consciousness in ordinary life:

> The inner freedom from the practical desire,
> The release from action and suffering, release from the inner
> And outer compulsion, yet surrounded
> By grace of sense, a white light still and moving

It is consciousness which abolishes fear of death, not so much because death becomes a passing to eternal home, but because eternal home is, to pick a phrase from *East Coker* out of context, "where one starts from" at every instant in the adventure of living, in this world or any other. The rest of my life adventure in this world is now dedicated to investigating possible other ways of breaking the enchainment of consciousness to past and future without dicing with death, or to coin a phrase, "How to Succeed into Eternity without Nearly Dying." I think this is humanity's great task for the coming millennium now that NDEs have shown us the possibility, and in that task I'm sure there is an enormous amount to be learned from the "guesses" of Thomas Stearns Eliot and his marvellous "raids on the inarticulate" in an effort to express them. And if I'm right about his heart attack in 1951, then his actual death in 1965 will have given a new twist of meaning to the lines which appear on his memorial in Westminster Abbey, taken from the last *Quartet*, the poem of fire called *Little Gidding* after the Huntingdonshire village he'd chosen for special prayers:

> And what the dead had no speech for, when living
> They can tell you, being dead: the communication
> Of the dead is tongued with fire beyond the language
>   of the living.

PROFESSOR JOHN WREN-LEWIS, a mathematical physicist well-known for his writings on science and spirituality, is now retired in Australia, where he is an honorary associate of the University of Sydney's School of Studies in Religion. His forthcoming book, *The 9:15 to Nirvana*, describes his near-death experience and resultant consciousness-change referred to here.

LORAINE CAMPBELL

Home on the Range

Herbert Haseltine. *Percheron*. Bronze and lapis. Collection of The University of Arizona Museum of Art, Tucson. Gift of Mrs. Fred Greiner, 1978.

"OH GIVE ME A HOME WHERE THE BUFFALO ROAM," my father sang as he rode in circles in the backyard, swinging his lariat.

We could hear the hammering of a house being built on the other side of our fence. The sounds of an electric saw drowned out his voice, but he went on swinging and singing.

"Here's the way the old timers did it," he called to my brother and me, with the rope whizzing and humming in circles about his head. Then he lassoed the gate post.

"Giddyap," he spoke to his horse, and bending down, they galloped under the clothesline. "Whoa," he spoke again gently, and the horse stopped.

Every night he came home from working as a salesman, set his briefcase on the dining room table, and changed from his business suit into his western shirt, jeans, and cowboy boots. *"Give me land, lots of land 'neath the starry skies above,"* he'd sing, as he headed for the back yard. *"Don't fence me in."*

My brother and I would run along behind him, watching as he saddled and bridled his horse.

"You're a fine old palomino," he'd say while patting, cinching, and buckling. Then he'd throw his arms around the horse's neck, and pat him some more.

After he'd mounted, he'd turn to us and say something important like: "'There's never a horse that couldn't be rode, and never a rider that couldn't be throwed.' That's what the old timers used to say."

Then he'd trot around doing figure eights between the rose bushes while asking us questions.

"Do you know what General Robert E. Lee said after Abraham Lincoln was assassinated?" he asked one day.

"No," I said.

"'I think the South has lost her best friend.'"

"Wow!" I said, then I paused. "Where's the South?" I asked, but he was circling the garbage cans and singing *"Oh play the fife lowly, beat the drums slowly, play the death march as you carry me along."*

"Where are you going?" asked my brother.

"Take me to the green valley and lay the sod o'er me...."

"Gee," we both said, frowning at each other.

"... for I'm a young cowboy and I know I've done wrong."

Sometimes he rode in front of the house, barium soles on the horse's feet clicking like castanets against the concrete. *"Home, home on the range, where the deer and the antelope play,"* he'd sing as he trotted down the street, dodging traffic.

One day a letter arrived in the mail from the City, informing my father that the little town we lived in was expanding its city limits to include our house, and more important, our backyard, which meant that my father could no longer stable his horses: "We regretfully inform you ... within the parameters and boundaries of said limits ... and furthermore, the defecation of large animals is offending the sensitivities of neighbors nearby, and causing horseflies to buzz through surrounding gardens, creating untold stress and inconvenience, and therefore within ninety days, said situation must cease thereof."

My father sold the house as fast as he could and bought a smaller house with a bigger yard, seven miles out of town. He pushed over a few prune trees and called the yard "the pasture." Then he built an electric fence which ticked day and night, picked up a few Aberdeen Angus cows, and called the pasture "the range."

When my mother heard that fence ticking, she asked my father if that's the way the old timers did it, but he ignored the question.

In the evenings after work he'd ride around in the yard singing: *"Git along little doggies; it's your misfortune and none of my own."*

The cows mooed and bumped into each other as they hurried to get out of his way, and he swung his lariat while he rode, but he didn't lasso them. He said it made them nervous.

Soon after that he started teaching me to ride. I was the oldest.

"Now the first thing you have to remember, Tweedie, is, you've got to have a good seat in the saddle. Some people don't. They're handicapped for life," he said. "They go up when the horse goes down, and come down when the horse goes up, and they're holding onto the horn for dear life. And you know," he said, shaking his head sadly, "there just doesn't seem to be anything anyone can do about it."

"Don't hold onto that horn!" he said to me when I climbed on my new pony and sat in my new saddle for the first time. "That's for tying your lariat. That's for when you're roping cattle!" I looked over at the few cows huddled against the fence, shaking their heads. They seemed to be talking about us.

"Oh, okay," I said. "But can I take my doll?"

"No!" said my father. "You're not playing. You're riding the range like the old timers."

I rode around and around in the yard, fiddling with the rope whenever my father wasn't watching. I tied it into a bow around the saddle horn, and tried to adjust my body to the horse's rhythm, the way the old timers did it. It wasn't hard, because that little pony was going as slow as she could.

"And another thing," my father called, "when you work with a horse, you have to talk to it. They all have feelings, just like us."

"Giddyap!" I said to the pony, but she ignored me. "Gidd-ee-up," I said again, louder. She turned her head and looked at me as if I were a fly. "C'mon," I whined, "go faster, you know what I mean!" But she slowed down and almost stopped.

"Give her a little nudge in the flanks," my father said. "Let her know who's boss. That's how the old timers did it."

I kicked a little with my brand new cowboy boots and silver spurs, and she started up again, bumping and stumbling like a car running out of gas.

We circled the yard, weaving in between the cows.

"Hold your reins with your left hand," my father said.

"But this is the hand I color with," I said, holding up my right.

"You need your right hand for swinging your lasso. You've got to be strong when you rope a steer."

"Oh, okay," I said, switching the reins.

My father rode along beside me. "*Ten thousand cattle strayed from my range,*" he sang.

"Well, Tweedie," he called. "Here we are riding across the prairie, just like the old timers."

My little brother came around the corner pulling his Teddy bear in his little red wagon.

"Gary Old Horse," my father called, "don't fire till you see the whites of their eyes."

"I wasn't going to," Gary said, frowning and staring at the bear, whose eyes were made of black buttons.

"And if they ask if you surrender, say, 'I've just begun to fight.'"

"OK," Gary said, touching the handle on his cap gun, which was swinging in a leather holster at his side.

He turned to the bear. "I've just begun to fight!" he said. "Giddyap!" Then he pulled the red wagon around the corner and out of sight.

We could stand in the pasture and see mountains in every direction. They changed colors during the day. Bees buzzed above the mustard flowers, and birds sang like an orchestra of piccolos, cellos, and flutes. When the moon was full, my brother and I could see an Easter Bunny with crooked ears in the center of it. Stars twinkled, and bull frogs croaked, a thousand at a time.

A creek rushed by in winter, sometimes washing the bridge away, and dried up in late spring. The pools of stagnant water got smaller and smaller, and by summer the polliwogs, the ones who hadn't become frogs yet, bumped into each other and swam in circles.

In the summer the horses poked their heads through the open windows and looked into our house. The big old palomino named Arizona licked my face tenderly whenever I had a fever.

My father washed Arizona's mane and tail with White Rain shampoo, and everyone laughed and said: "Is that the way the old timers did it?"

My father went on scrubbing, added some blueing solution for extra whiteness, and accidentally changed the color of the horse's tail.

"Drifting along with the tumbling tumble weeds," my father sang, crushing mustard and clover under the horse's hoofs. *"The devil take the blue-tail fly."*

One day we heard a hammer pounding, then an electric saw. Trees began to fall. The land on the other side of our fence had been sold.

Someone started a business painting cars, and machines whined and screeched. Power lawn mowers roared early in the morning, and the rototillers and cutters chewed up the ground and spit it out.

A bulldozer came, and a couple of tractors, and they fiddled around, grinding and groaning; and when they left, the creek was made of cement, the polliwogs were buried alive, and the water ran all year in the opposite direction.

The orchards around us were sold—apple trees, cherry, and prune—and they were pushed over, cracking and creaking, and stacked like trash before the huge machines carted them away.

Apartments were built; pink and grey rooftops with aluminum window frames and television antennas blocked our view of the mountains.

Then one day a letter came, saying that the town we lived in was expanding its limits to include our house, and more importantly, our backyard. "The defecation of large animals, the mooing and neighing, is offending the sensitivities of surrounding neighbors, causing untold stress and inconvenience, and therefore, within 90 days, said situation must cease, thereof."

My father sold the horses and cows. Trailers pulled into our yard, and Ringo, Topper, Clancy, Buck and Arizona were loaded inside.

I ran along behind as they were driven away, waving and calling good-bye. There were tears in my eyes, and I was sure the horses were crying too. We never saw any of them again.

Then my father sold some of the land to keep up with the new taxes. We could see a clothesline in someone's backyard, where the corral used to be.

The moon was just as bright, but my brother and I couldn't see the Easter Bunny with the crooked ears anymore. We were too old.

Bees still buzzed in the gardens, but the mustard, poppy and clover were gone, and everything was neatly spaced and planted in a row.

We could hear birds occasionally, when the lawn mowers were quiet, and for a while, a couple of leftover bull frogs got in a croak or two.

My father stopped singing. In the evenings after work, he'd set his briefcase on the dining room table, and read books about the Wild West, the Civil War, the Battle of Manassas, and Custer's Last Stand.

Once in a while he'd look up from a page and ask something like: "Did you ever hear what General Robert E. Lee said after Abraham Lincoln was assassinated?"

"No, what?" one of us would ask.

"'I think the South has lost her best friend.'"

He'd shake his head sadly. Then he'd read some more. After a while he'd look up again.

"And did you know that Stonewall Jackson was shot by one of his own guards. They called them pickets . . ."

"Why, no," we'd say.

"Yes," he'd continue, "and when he lay on the ground dying, he said: 'Let us cross the river and rest in the shade of the trees.'"

"Wow!" I'd say. "Then what happened?"

"Beat the drums slowly, play the fife lowly."

LORRAINE CAMPBELL began writing after years of being an amateur painter and reports that she has learned two key principles: keep it simple and stay close to the heart. Her stories have appeared in *Grit*, *The Sun*, *Aim*, and *Writing for our Lives*, as well as in the Chrysalis Reader.

ROBERT BLY

The Hills Near Darky, Wisconsin

We are nearing those stumpy hills
Near Darky, with oaks on top.
Brown leaves surround each oak trunk,
Like something seen in deep sleep.
I grow dizzy and do not know why.
Round hills, a spring green on the slopes,
Becoming brown at the top,
Rising from the wintry cornfields.

Nicolai Clkovsky.
Wisconsin Landscape.
Oil on canvas, 1941.
Collection of The University
of Arizona Museum
of Art , Tucson. Gift
of C. Leonard Pfeiffer.

ROBERT BLY's most current books are *Eating the Honey Words: New and Selected Poems* (HarperCollins), *The Lightning Should Have Fallen on Ghalib: Selected Poems of Ghalib* (Ecco, translated with Sunil Dutta), and *The Best American Poetry* 1999 (Scribner).

JOSEPH H. FOEGEN AND SUSAN FOEGEN

Growing Up in Wisconsin

Reminiscences of Mother and Son

SUSAN: I was born in 1896. Until my early teens, I lived in a small town in Wisconsin, the youngest of a family of six. I lived alone most of that time with my widowed mother, a native of Germany. She spoke that country's language at first. I'd answer in English; later, she could speak English too.

She would take a walk to the cemetery every evening—it was only a block away, at what was then the edge of town—and I would go with her. She would meet friends there, I would too, and we would visit. It was a different, less-hectic lifestyle, compared with today's.

JOSEPH: Later on, we kids liked to go along on these cemetery visits. Missing the significance of the place, we saw it as a big park in which to play hide-and-seek among the headstones. The question of why that huge expanse of soft green grass was scattered with all those hunks of rock escaped us.

Another thing hard to figure was why two, widely separated plots needed attention on each visit. We learned later that it concerned mother's and father's relatives, respectively. For others, ethnic differences were sometimes responsible for separated plots, but not for us. Both sides of the family were German through and through.

When older, I worked at the cemetery part time during summers, helping the caretaker (another relative!) cut those grassy acres. He usually did the wide open spaces, while I had to cut around each stone with a hand mower (weedeaters were far in the future). Tedium was relieved somewhat by studying the fascinating old dates on the markers. It was the start of a more-than-casual interest in "roots."

SUSAN: At age seven, I started school. In those days, this meant reading, writing, and 'rithmetic. No parties! School ended at four o'clock, and then I had chores to do at home: fill the wood box, carry in water, haul stove coal into the house, and empty the ash pan. All these jobs were done before supper. After the meal, I was ready for bed at eight, another difference from the way most children live today. After eight grades I graduated and got no more formal education.

JOSEPH: While Susan did have little formal schooling, her native intelligence made up for that. During the little time available when not doing household chores, she read as much as possible, often aloud to us kids, and encouraged us to do the same. My favorite book at the time was *Grimm's Fairy Tales;* my repeated selection was called "If I Could Only Learn to Shudder."

The Milwaukee Journal was received six times weekly, the hometown *Kaukauna Times* twice. A cousin brought comics from *The Chicago Tribune* regularly, and many were instructive. History came from the long-running "Prince Valiant," vocabulary, and folk wisdom from many others.

From all these sources and more, from radio and active association with friends and neighbors, Susan got an unofficial, but effective education that made the "only eight grades" misleading. Creating a learning environment, whether deliberate or intuitive, paid off in more than one way. She saw both sons graduate from the University of Wisconsin. Her husband Henry should get credit, too. Equally supportive, he received the equivalent of a high-school education, in a parentally pushed but failed effort aimed at the priesthood.

SUSAN: For "entertainment," I painted small pictures, read books, and visited with a friend who lived nearby. Both painting and visiting were lifelong pastimes.

JOSEPH: Working mostly in watercolors, Susan produced many scenic views, among them mill streams, churches, and snowscapes. Most were done from memory, some from magazine illustrations. More unique, many of her weekly letters for almost half a century were hand illustrated, as befitted the season or topic. Many efforts were both elaborate and creative.

A common and pleasant diversion in those "low-tech" days before TV and widespread car ownership, "visiting" was an extended pleasure. Most houses then boasted large front porches, including ours. People walked, not for exercise, but of necessity. Relatives often lived nearby. They, neighbors, and friends would stroll past in the evenings and would hear routinely, "Come up and sit for a while." Such socializing was the Internet of its day!

Our own porch also served as a neighborhood bandshell, the venue of many impromptu concerts. Family members played by ear rather than from printed music, on accordion, mandolin, guitar, and harmonica in various combinations. When the first strains were heard, neighborhood kids came running from all directions, as with Hamelin's Pied Piper.

SUSAN: I worked briefly at a local mill that made paper bags, but after a few months was laid off and never went back.

JOSEPH: For employment, the local paper mill was for decades the "only game in town." Founded by a German immigrant, Thilmany Pulp & Paper Company saw generations of city residents earn their bread there. Some worked on log cranes, chippers, beaters, and digesters in the pulping process. Others monitored and maintained block-long paper machines that ran constantly except for a few weeks of summer shutdowns for maintenance. Still others put in their "daily dozens" on presses, embossers, trimmers, and wax and asphalt laminating machines that turned out specialty packaging products. When union workers finally achieved a wage of a dollar an hour, it was considered a major accomplishment.

A television weather channel was as unnecessary as it was nonexistent. When residents' noses detected the pulp mill's characteristic rotten-eggs odor, it meant the wind was in the East and the pressure was falling. Rain or snow followed invariably. Though the sulphurous smell clung to both clothes and skin and offended visitors to our city, locals didn't mind. "The Mill" was running—something experience proved could not be taken for granted—producing both jobs and income.

Ahead of its time, Susan's employer hired many women, mostly for two jobs. They worked on bag machines that spewed product rapidly. They also removed buttons and other foreign matter from the rags used to make high-quality, cotton-fiber paper. Women were assumed to have greater hand and finger dexterity than men. They would also work for less money, since their jobs were typically supplemental and temporary.

SUSAN: Meanwhile, my mother sold our house, and we moved two and a half miles from town to a farm to help my brother, who owned it and was still single. I lived there ten years.

Vowing at first never to milk cows, I finally did anyway—more than a *few* too! One was especially hard to milk. After getting a full pail from her one evening, I felt proud of myself. But she "got the last squirt" anyway. Picking up one foot, she put it smack-dab into the pailful of good milk. I was "madder than a wet hen" at having to pour all that hard-to-come-by milk down the gutter.

I did manage to attend some dances in town, usually riding in with my brother, but then being on my own. The band played different kinds of music, of course, but waltzes were my favorite. I met my future husband at one such outing. He was an excellent dancer, so we didn't miss many opportunities. A waltz with "Heinie" (Henry) was perfect. Later, we married—September 12, 1923—and lived in a new home he had built for us.

JOSEPH: A four-bedroom, two-story frame structure, it was painted white through its entire history. Built during the Depression era when jobs and money were scarce, it attested to white paint's being least expensive. Later, it became habit. Creativity was limited to trim color, although habit prevailed here too. The color was always green.

The house stood on the corner of Desnoyer and Ducharme Streets, named for early French explorers. The Chicago Northwestern Railroad's main tracks were only a block and half away. Both freight and—in those days—passenger trains shuttled between Chicago, Milwaukee, and Green Bay. Even at a distance of almost two blocks, the house shook noticeably when one went by. At night, when all else was quiet, the plaintive "whoo-ee" of the train blowing for highway crossings, was somehow appealing. Finally, however, after almost seventy years of life and memories, the house had to be sold (see "Goodbye to the Child Home," *Catalyst*, Summer, 1993).

SUSAN: One Sunday, my "beau"—as special men friends were often called in those days—rented a horse and top-buggy to come and get me, and on the way home I lost my hat. The top was tipped back, the curtain had been open unknown to us, and my hat fell through the opening. I could just picture that bonnet later, rolling down the road to who knows where!

I also recall vividly a winter trip with horse and cutter (sleigh). The cutter tipped, trying to turn into the land near our house, and the horse galloped away with it, while I watched helplessly from the snow bank where I landed. No bruises, though. The cutter soon got hung up on the clothes pole in our yard, and was damaged. Unfairly, my "one-and-only" had to *walk* home, and even pay for repairs. I never heard how big the bill was, and didn't ask!

Making hay was another major part of farming during those years. Often I helped, setting up bundles, or using a big rake pulled by a horse to gather it from the fields. Occasionally, one of the big wheels would get caught in a fence, and it was quite a job trying to free it.

One day while making hay, a storm was brewing, and my brother wanted to haul the dry hay in before the storm broke. I was on the hayrack driving the team, and everyone in the crew was hurrying. In an unexpectedly strong gust, the wind toppled the rack off the wagon and me with it! My brother was so excited when the rack tipped, he fell to the ground himself and couldn't move for a while.

We kept geese, and the gander we had was really mean. He would give chase any time or place he saw you. My mother once got cornered in the outside cellar entrance while trying to escape the pest.

In the barn upstairs, we had a swing secured to the top of the granary. Before the gaping empty space below was filled with hay, it excited us kids to swing back and forth over it.

We may have been poor by some standards, but we were neat. I took some credit for that, keeping the lawn and barnyard free of stray boards and other junk. Praise from the neighbors was my reward.

My mother cooked, baked, and took care of chickens. One bird was a bit nosy and once stuck her head into an empty can and couldn't get it out. Mother picked up the can and shook it until the chicken fell down and ran away. That was another sight to behold!

JOSEPH: In those days, eating chicken was considered something special. Its table appearance was reserved for Sunday dinner, the week's high point, or for holidays. President Herbert Hoover's ideal of a "chicken in every pot" was symbolic of the luxury of everyone having enough to eat.

When feasting on chicken was to be enjoyed, it meant not a trip to the local supermarket, there to choose from a large display of plastic-wrapped cuts. Rather, it meant *catching* one of those very agile birds, taking it to the basement (at *our* house), decapitating the struggling victim, gutting it, soaking the carcass in boiling water to loosen feathers, and plucking them. Only then was it ready for kitchen preparation and roasting. Today, one wonders whether it was worth all that effort. Made "from scratch" by a skilled cook like Susan, however, and regardless of hard work, the result was delicious.

SUSAN: My sister and family visited from Appleton on weekends occasionally. Before cars were common, a 15-mile round-trip took a lot of effort. Sunday, we all rode to church on the milk wagon, as we called it. My mother, brother, and brother-in-law sat on the seat, while my sister and I sat on the back end, legs hanging over the end. One time, my brother was driving fast and went over a bump, jolting my sister and me up off the wagon bed. The wagon kept going while we, obeying gravity, landed in the road, surprised for sure, but "none the worse for the wear." When about half a block ahead, the others finally noticed we were missing on the wagon. They waited for us to catch up. We all had a good laugh!

All these random memories probably sound hopelessly old-fashioned to younger readers. Nevertheless, I would never trade them for today's typical routines. The life was not easy, it's true, and the only labor-saving devices were at the ends of your arms. Still the down-to-earth living—literally as well as figuratively!—was satisfying overall and rewarding in its own way.

JOSEPH H. FOEGEN is a professor of business at Winona State University. His byline has appeared in several hundred articles in a wide range of professional and other publications. His mother, SUSAN FOEGEN, lived to the age of ninety-six and wrote almost until the end of her life, hand-illustrating most pieces as you see here. She also played the mandolin, baked homemade bread, and, her son says, made "mouth-watering lemon-meringue pies from scratch."

THOMAS KRETZ

Pittsburgh in 1950

That was back when snow blackened
in ten minutes from soot and smog
sometimes thicker than London fog.
Usually disgustingly healthy starlings

and crows coughed blood on our side
of town. Trains made passengers weep.
Policemen were so bored they spent
whole evenings looking in boxcars
for a hobo or an illegal game of poker;
murders and muggings rare as wine.

My older brother and I just picked at
fried green tomatoes and spare ribs,
watching our parents down Iron City
beer over our rims of liquid cholesterol.
We would have gobbled the ribs down
with Pepsi to get back to the ball game
that kept the local playground occupied
from dawn to dusk every season of the year,
but only sister could do as she pleased
so we dallied until a parent said: Scram!

Though the Pirates and Steelers always
lurked in league cellars we pretended we
were two of their best to make a difference
next year. Just wait. We did. Championships
never held any interest for Pittsburgh boys.
The Catholic grade school was two miles
from home. No one thought of riding. In
eight years I never saw one parent bring
a child, pick one up. My brother and I had
good friends, cried when we had to move.

Born in Pittsburgh, THOMAS KRETZ has worked for the past twenty-five years in Europe as an historian and accountant. He presently manages a home for elderly Jesuits.

LANI WRIGHT

Silent Messenger

FROM A DISTANCE, the luna moth lying at the side of the road, its lime green a bright smear of color against the black tarmac, looked like a large spring leaf torn loose in a thunderstorm. But it turned out to be another kind of fragile, another kind of separation. I knelt down to see if it were dead or alive. No sign of movement until I turned it gently. Then its feathery antlers began to dance back and forth as if it were trying to tell me something. Its hairy body cavity had been torn open and its miniature insect organs were spilling out, probably from impacting some large steel and glass monster being driven forward at impossibly dangerous speeds. Everyday I pray to my guardian angels to protect me from a similar end as I pass this way on rollerblades, largely unprotected, only inches from their missile strength. So far so good for me, though not for this beautiful moth. Moths do not take care along roadways. They do not look both ways before they cross. They flutter wherever the sweet breeze takes them or the scent of blossoms lure.

The sun was cooking the pavement. I lifted the weightless body and placed it in a nearby mailbox where it would be shaded and less buffeted from the backdraft of passing tractor trailer trucks. Later, I drove back to bring it home to die under my flowering begonia next to a cotton ball soaked in water. The dying thirst. I know this. I remember my mother at the end—her mouth a leathery red 0. Her lips cracked and peeling. The dying gulp in big pillows of dry air and gasp out the precious moisture that is their life.

It took a day and a half for the moth to die. Meanwhile the rains came again. All night they rattled my screens and shook the roof. In the morning, as I walked the dog at daybreak, I passed my neighbor outside in his pajamas and slippers, getting soaked as he pruned lilac and wigelia away from his porch steps with a pair of big loppers. I had to laugh because I have done the same thing. Only it looked sillier watching someone else do it. I know it's only when the shrubbery is soaked and you have to brush against it on your way to gather the morning paper that you think to find clippers. When the sun is out, all that greenery only looks pleasingly wild draped over the entranceway.

Now as I read all the sad stories delivered daily to my home, I think of how our species must learn to make connections and act while the sun is shining, but, of course, we don't. We procrastinate. I think of the ozone layer slowly losing weight. Maybe things will fix themselves if we wait long enough . . . I hear the crash and drip of polar caps melting into the sea. Maybe somebody else will take care of it. I see the impossibly high smoke stacks which send their acids half a continent away to kill the maple trees in my backyard. We have a tendency to hope.

It will be a day of mourning when there are no luna moths left. The insects will be the last to go, disappearing forever long after the large huntable mammals who need great habitats, like we do. For as we all know, it's not enough to have our house, our garage, our garden, and our yard. We need golf courses and shopping malls and larger speedy-smooth highways to link them all together so we can dash even more rapidly from activity to activity in the race that is our lives—never stopping to enjoy the things we've already bought. Or so it seems most days.

I put the newspaper into the recycling bin and go outside to check on the moth whose life drifts away on its last out breath. I offer up a moth-sized prayer for its spirit and carry it inside on a white porcelain tray.

Since then I've been worshipping its wings which are as sweet and graceful as a child's face. When I look at them under my slide magnifier, which increases things to eight times their size, and look right down into the purple eye, it's like falling into an M. C. Escher drawing. It's like entering a maze full of false starts and occasional dead ends, and through-passageways too, if only we can find them.

LANI WRIGHT has been an outdoor educator, language teacher, and college administrator. Her voice has been heard reading commentary on travel, nature, and women and spirituality on National Public Radio's Morning Edition through member affiliate station WFCR in Amherst, Massachusetts. Her personal essays have been published in the Chrysalis Reader, *Out of the Kitchen,* and *The Sun,* and as opinion pieces in the *Brattleboro Reformer.*

JAMES RENSENBRINK

The Seaman

Alone with a gargantuan rage at death
the merchant seaman walked on water for hours.
He had momentarily discovered his lightness
because of a coincidence of damaged colors, he said,
but everyone he talked to agreed that, sooner or later,
he would drown anyway, so why bother?
He longed to tell them he had become swifter
and more brilliant than terror and thereby knew
some things—that Autumn's forests were not an accident,
for instance, but a hint of the masterpiece—
but in America credentials had to be present for anyone
to be heard about anything and he had none of them.
Little birds, however, were utterly indifferent
to his whinings, and told him that by finding the sea of air
he would learn how to swim, and once swimming, would disappear
into a sea of color and once there—
reflecting colors which strangely had always been his—
he too would become indifferent,
not even remembering either his rage or his name.
Nights of darkness, they said, swimming into flame.

JAMES RENSENBRINK is currently working on three novels, a philosophic work called *The Nature of Knowing*, and a book of poems, due out this year. He is the editor and publisher of a yearly publication called *Sha-People*. He lives in Montclair, New Jersey.

PART VI

Through a Mirror Darkly

SARAH VOSS

Going Beyond Copernicus

HOW DID THE UNIVERSE COME INTO BEING? The latest creation hypothesis is the "Big Bang theory." According to this scientific myth, the universe was created about fifteen billion years ago from a great, probably expanding, but ultimately mysterious explosion. With this explosion, time came into existence, followed by hydrogen and helium, and, much later, stars and us. Well, stars and us didn't exactly arrive in the same sentence, but it's definitely the correct chronology. Not everybody currently believes the Big Bang theory, but most "educated" people do.

In fact, there have been many different versions of the creation of the universe. What is of particular interest to me is the corre-

Patrick J. Sullivan. *The Fourth Dimension.* Oil on canvas, 24¼×30¼ in., 1938. The Museum of Modern Art, New York. The Sidney and Harriet Janis Collection. Photograph ©2000 The Museum of Modern Art, New York.

> Donald MacKay, British biophysicist and world authority on brain physiology, writing in the 1980s about the nature of God:
> *Imagine now an artist able to bring his world into being, not by laying down paint on a canvas, but by producing an extremely rapid succession of sparks of light on the screen of a television tube.... The world he invents is now not static but dynamic, able to change and evolve at his will. Both its form and its laws of change (if any) depend on the way in which he orders the sparks of light in space and time. With one sequence he produces a calm landscape with quietly rolling clouds; with another, we are looking at a vigorous cricket match on a village green. The scene is steady and unchanging just for as long as he wills it so; but if he were to cease his activity, his invented world would not become chaotic; it would simply cease to be.*
> THE GOD WHO WOULD BE KNOWN: REVELATIONS OF THE DIVINE IN CONTEMPORARY SCIENCE, by John M. Templeton and Robert L. Herrmann San Francisco: Harper & Row, 1989, page 21.

sponding views of the cosmos which these assorted legends reflected. *Enuma Elish*, the Babylonian creation myth, reveals a two-layer universe. When the god Marduk split Tiamat in half with his ax, he separated her body into an upper heaven and a lower earth. Eastern tradition often depicts a three-layer universe—a flattened disk that is earth, the atmosphere of rain and wind, and the sun and fire of the heavens crowning it all. To the ancient Greeks (ca. 6th century BCE), the earth was likewise a flattened disk, but the sun and stars were masses of fire, surrounded by air, and flung to the perimeter of this disk. Both the sun and moon were shaped like huge solar chariot wheels, twenty-eight and nineteen times the size of the earth, respectively.[1]

Sometimes these early cosmogonies (explanations of the origin of the world) were also theogonies (explanations of the origins of the gods). In general, the cosmological "map" of ancient times depicted the world as a bubble with the deities in the heavens at the top of the sphere, the earthly creatures below, and a temple of some sort with a king in between. The Deity, who kept the waters of chaos at bay, quite literally resided in the upper firmament, which was held up by the mountains. Since the distance between the earth and the top of the mountains was relatively small (maybe a mile and a half), the Deity might well come down to the earth, or you might even see him (or her) on a mountain.

By the time of Aristotle (ca. 350 BCE), the sun, planets, and stars were all attached to rigid spheres which circled a static earth. Variations on this map occurred, with 7, 8, 144, and sometimes 365 spherical layers surrounding an earth which remained pointedly in the center of a bubble-like universe. The Deity, however, resided outside these concentric layers—no more going up to the mountaintop for a visit. In fact, the best way to commune with the Deity was to go into a vision or dream, ascend these various spheres, then descend to tell others. Alternatively, the Deity might come down into the cosmos; that could happen, though, only if he put on a body, a somewhat risky proposition in that he might get trapped down here, which was a most undesirable possibility since the earth was a dark, stinky, spiritually bereft place. Thus, in this cosmology, God becomes a utopian image, and life becomes an attempt to break out of the confines of an ugly physical world.

SOME FOUR-HUNDRED FIFTY YEARS AGO, beginning with the Polish astronomer Copernicus, the cosmological map changed again. The earth lost its position of centrality, and the sun took its place. The circling earth and planets were still spatially bound by an unchanging outer rim of fixed stars, but eventually this ridgidity changed, too. Today, we recognize our sun as only one of countless stars moving through a changing universe in somewhat chaotic patterns. Copernicus started a theological revolution marked by the "heretical" view that the earth was no longer at the center of the universe. This meant humans were no longer at the center either. This change was met with resistance. To some extent, it is still being met with resistance. Note, for instance, the emergence in recent years of the anthropic principle.[2] One contemporary cosmologist, Michio Kaku, puts it this way: "Within the past few decades, some cosmologists have been horrified to find anthropomorphism creeping back into science under the guise of the anthropic principle, some of whose advocates openly declare that they would like to put God back into science."[3] The idea is that there had to be a creator of this well-designed world, and that creator, of course, is God.

The anthropic principle is but one outcome of our present-day "big bang" cosmogony. This cosmogony explains our contemporary map of the universe, which holds that the earth is one of several planets revolving about one of countless stars in a galaxy of stars, which is only one of countless galaxies strewn chaotically, but for a finite time, across an infinite but possibly bounded universe. This map corresponds fairly accurately to the physical data we are presently able to collect with our assorted measuring instruments.

The map that accompanies this emerging cosmogony resembles a kaleidoscope more than a universe of meandering galaxies. The meandering galaxies and the universe as we know it haven't disappeared. Rather, this familiar depiction is only one of many patterns which a kaleidoscope holds within its illusion-producing mirror-walls. The metaphor I have in mind as a map of the universe is not as simplistic as an ordinary kaleidoscope. The chief difference is that it is a nonphysical *thought* kaleidoscope reflecting, amplifying, and creating symbols. The three-dimensional kaleidoscopes we are familiar with usually contain some kind of colorful beads or glass chips. Strategically located mirrors and/or lenses reflect these beads, turning them into elaborate designs. In our *living* kaleidoscope these

---

Cassius Jackson Keyser, mathematician, writing in the 1930s about the nature of the universe:
[T]he whole world of physical facts—space, time, rivers, rocks, plant bodies, animal bodies, atoms, stars, nebulae—is just an immense and complicated system of symbols continually made, unmade, and remade by mind (soul, spirit), in response to the natural needs of mind, to represent, without copying or resembling, activities of mind. Mind is the sole Reality, all else—the external universe—being only a mind-required, mind-made, mind-sustained, mind-symbolizing, mind-revealing Pageant.
MATHEMATICS AND THE QUESTION
OF THE COSMIC MIND
WITH OTHER ESSAYS
New York: Scripta Mathematica, 1935, pp. 61–62.

> Robert Ornstein, contemporary consciousness researcher, writing on how the mind is a "world-processing system":
>
> *The world we experience, all the horses, the leaves, the coffee, the sunrises, the remembrance of things past, is all a dream of the mind. And more, for the mind is filled with different dreamers, some of whom don't know about each other. They contradict each other, as dreamers do.*
>
> THE EVOLUTION OF CONSCIOUSNESS
> New York: Prentice Hall, 171

beads or chips are replaced by the three-dimensional artifacts of ordinary reality. They—we—are "symbols" reflected into intricate patterns by mind (or soul or spirit).

The "thought is all there is" notion is really very old. However, late twentieth century insights, particularly in physics and mathematics, suggest that we should dust off this old metaphor and give it contemporary clothing. What are these recent insights? I will mention here several of the more pertinent.

In 1927, a scientific revelation known as the Heisenberg uncertainty principle showed that we can never observe the velocity and the position of a subatomic particle simultaneously. If we know one of these properties, we can only predict the other according to the probabilities of chance. Subsequently it was discovered that this principle applies to other quantum properties as well. For example, certain particles are known to spin either clockwise or counterclockwise with equal probability, but until the spin is actually calculated (observed), there is no way of telling which spin it has. In other words, both spins are somehow latent within the particle and it is only the act of observation which determines it. This amazing notion resulted from the combined efforts of a number of gifted scientists working in the early 1900s, including Werner Heisenberg, Niels Bohr, P.A.M. Dirac, Albert Einstein, Erwin Schrödinger, Max Planck, and Louis De Broglie.

The discovery of the Heisenberg uncertainty principle and its related implications met with resistance even among the discoverers. Nonetheless, the uncertainty principle has now been experimentally verified repeatedly and has had the effect of displacing, once and for all, the Newtonian world-vision of clock-like order and predictability with one dominated by uncertainty and chance. One contemporary scientist even held that while it is one of the silliest theories proposed in this century, quantum theory is unquestionably correct.

A recent variation of this uncertainty principle has cropped up in the macroscopic realm of the cosmologists. Known as the multi-universe theory, the basic tenet is that our universe is only one of many potential universes which are latent within creation. Actually, there are several physical theories that imply the existence of an ensemble of universes, but, in general, the various universes might be considered in some sense "parallel" or coexisting realities. Bizarre as this seems, many physicists and some philosophers support some version of the multi-universe theory.[4] Today there is even growing popular awareness of what is called the quantum vacuum—a nonempty void, which holds the probabilistic potential for everything. The notion gives a new and very pluralistic meaning to the concept of creation out of nothing.

The development of simulated and virtual realities, recent advances in cognitive science and neuroscience, and ideas stemming from the mathematical theories of complexity, holography, and hyperspace are further stimulating this emerging sense of multiple-existence. For instance, M.I.T. psychologist Sherry Turkel observes that our sense of self is becoming more "consciously multiple" because of the Net. Computers are affecting our ideas about mind, body, self, and machine, she writes. Virtual reality games known as Multi-User Domains (MUDs) allow individuals to take on other personalities, some of which become so important that real life begins to lose its significance. A college student describes it this way: "I split my mind. I'm getting better at it. I can see myself as being two or three or more. And I just turn on one part of my mind and then another when I go from window to window."[5] The current film industry incorporates this notion of virtual existences into popular movies such as *Matrix, The Thirteenth Floor,* and *ExistenZ,* where, accompanied by all sorts of ethical questions, it is gradually seeping into the collective consciousness of modern culture.

To cite another instance and from what he depicts as *The Holographic Universe,* Michael Talbot writes that "the tangible reality of our everyday lives is really a kind of illusion," grounded by a much deeper and more primary order of existence.[6] In this perspective, drawn from the theory of Einstein's protégé, David Bohm, consciousness is a subtle form of matter, the observer *is* the observed, the line of separation between animate and inanimate life becomes blurred, the distinction between past and future is an illusion, and "every cell in our body enfolds the entire cosmos."[7] Thus Bohm's holography, which originally appeared as nothing more than abstract mathematical equations, gave rise to a "dynamic and kaleidoscopic" world—one that is "not really there."[8] Reality, in this depiction, is nebulous and nonlocal.

To mention one final example, physicist Saul-Paul Sirag has developed a theory of consciousness which is based on mathematical structures called *reflection spaces*. In an interview on national public television, Sirag recalled his own journey: "When I was in college maybe twenty years ago, people talked about maybe there were more than three dimensions, but then they kind of laughed it off. Now physicists take the notion of hyperspace, or multiple dimensions of reality, as being matter-of-fact."[9] When Sirag describes his hyperspace view of consciousness, he uses the same words, symbols, and connections that appear in highly specialized contemporary mathematics textbooks: McKay groups, Lie algebra, permutation classes, eigenvector equations, etc. By using these mathematical tools, Sirag insists that he is "describing the spiritual realm." "Obviously," he adds, "most physicists don't take this point of view yet, but I think they will in another couple of decades."[10]

Space constraints limit my mentioning additional theories that go "beyond Copernicus." Hopefully, the sidebar quotes provide some sense of contemporary voices lending support to a kaleidoscopic view. Coming from different areas of interest and study, these assorted viewpoints all suggest that our modern cosmogony may be changing. The best map of reality appears to be multiple, shifting, and to some degree uncertain.

ESSENTIALLY, MY SUGGESTION IS THAT THE COPERNICAN VIEWPOINT (that our earth circles a sun which is only one of many stars within a universe filled with galaxies of stars, etc.) is inaccurate. It is far too narrow and restricted a view, although, admittedly, it has served us well for its duration, just as the Ptolemaic map worked pretty well for its duration. Nonetheless, the Copernican understanding might be better replaced with a "Kaleidoscopic" viewpoint, wherein the Copernican "map" is only one of an infinity of possible designs. It is not just that our universe as we know it, with all its experimentally verified Copernican features, might itself be part of a multi-universe-design. Rather, the entire physical framework is an illusion; it is but one of an infinity of possible kaleidoscopic designs.

In this model, Spirit (God Mind) exists as one undifferentiated whole, but it only manifests itself in fragmented parts, parts which are actually "symbols" for Spirit. These, in turn, are "mirrored" in some fashion, which is the way Spirit can know itself. That is, these fragmented symbols of Spirit are in constant (but changing) relationship to each other, and their organization is the creative, competent, intelligent aspect of Spirit at work. This creativity may manifest itself in the tables, clouds, stars, animals, humans, etc., of our familiar physical world, but it may manifest itself in totally different ways as well, ways belonging to some other dimension of hyperspace, so to speak. With every "turn" of Spirit, a new universe comes into being. This does not mean that the other aspects of Spirit no longer exist: just as some of the colored beads in a kaleidoscope disappear from sight but not from existence, so, too, does Spirit selectively reveal itself.

Such, then, is the pluralistic model of reality I set before you here. What does this have to do with how we live our lives? To be sure, I believe some important ethical considerations follow, but they must wait for another essay. It is enough here to re-emphasize the heavily relational characteristic of this model. All is relationship. For we are fragmented parts of a collective Spirit, existing in intimate and dynamic relationship to each other. That is,

> We are the words She writes
> by joining cells one to another
> as we set letters side by side, form shapes
> that stand for meanings rarely understood.
>
> Like marks that decorate
> the sheets of dictionaries,
> we hold no weight, bear no substance,
> live lives as simple symbols
> strung together into lines—
> ever changing colloquialisms
> reflecting patterns
> we call definitions, and yet
>
> sometimes we rearrange ourselves
> in ways that please Her eye:
> sentences in books that charm,
> turn abstracts into loved designs
> soon viewed as wondrous tales.

Notes

1. See, for example, Lightman, Alan, *Ancient Light: Our Changing View of the Universe* (Cambridge, Harvard University Press, 1991), pp. 5–10.
2. Presented in both *strong* and *weak* versions, the anthropic principle says, essentially, that, given the infinite multitude of possible worlds that might have developed with the big bang and given the extreme sensitivity of the initial physical constants needed in order for a world such as ours to exist, the very fact that we do exist means that the universe more-or-less *had* to happen the way it has happened. The fact that the universe exists in its present form is a reflection of our own existence, and is, thus, dependent upon human existence.
3. Kaku, Michio, *Hyperspace* (New York: Doubleday, 1994), 257. Another useful source of information about theology and the anthropic principle is Paul Davies, *The Mind of God: The Scientific Basis for a Rational World* (New York: Simon and Schuster, 1992).
4. Davies, p. 217.
5. Turkle, Sherry, *Life on the Screen: Identity in the Age of the Internet* (New York: Simon and Schuster, 1995).
6. Talbot, Michael, *The Holographic Universe* (New York: HarperCollins, 1991), p. 46.
7. *Ibid.,* p. 50.
8. Ferguson, Marilyn, *The Aquarian Conspiracy* (Los Angeles: J.P.Tarcher, 1980), p. 180.
9. Mishlove, Jeffrey, *Thinking Allowed: Conversations on the Leading Edge of Knowledge* (Tulsa: Council Oak Books, 1992), p. 105.
10. *Ibid.,* p. 108.

SARAH VOSS is a Unitarian–Universalist minister, lecturer, and author. Among her books are *What Number Is God?* (SUNY, 1995) and *Zero: Reflections About Nothing* (CrossCultural Publications, 1998). She has also published over a hundred poems and articles. She is currently writing a novel and also turning material from her award-winning class, "Math: A New Language of Theology," into a religious-education curriculum.

RITA QUINTON

Good for Business

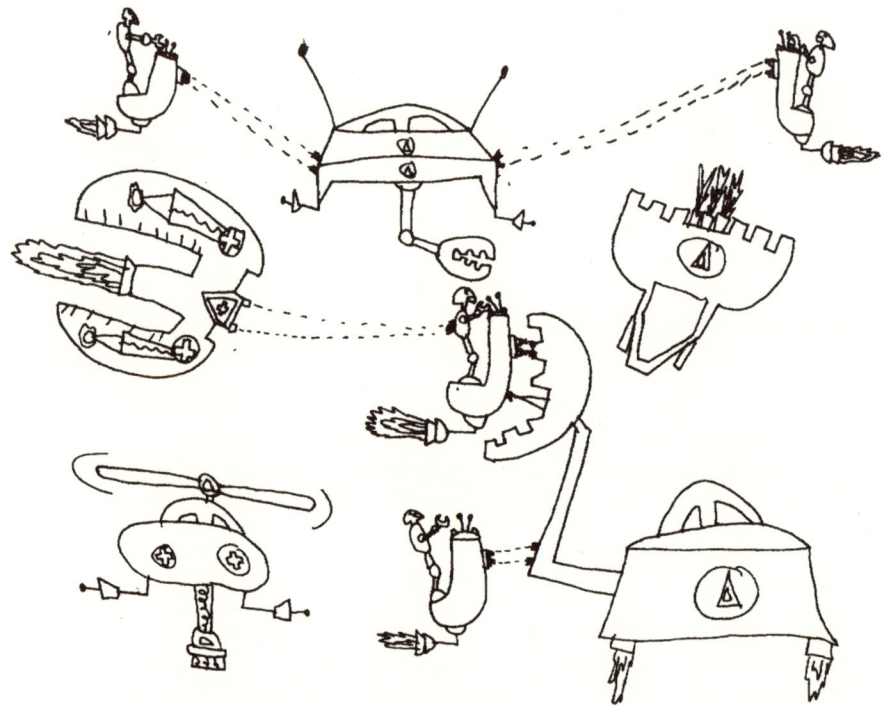

Christopher Batchelder (seven-years-old). *Space Doodles.* Pen-and-ink, 2000.

HE'D TAKE TWO GRIEF PILLS FOR THE FUNERAL. Selena had been a good wife for twenty years. It was the least he could do for her, and for himself. It would not do for the general public to suspect him of not using his own products, but the thought of all the tears and sobs two pills would generate made him queasy. Perhaps one pill would suffice.

Ms. Claridge entered the spacious office. She was her usual self, Darren Eberle noted with satisfaction. Trust Ms. Claridge to know better than to take a Compassion Pill as so many of his other employees had seen fit to do when they heard of Selena's death. There were no tears, but the gloomy, solemn attitude generated by the pill definitely interfered with their work.

"I've made all the arrangements," she said in her crisp way. "The viewing will be this evening. A blanket of roses and a large heart of orchids have been ordered, 'Beloved Wife' on both. Small service at the funeral parlor tomorrow morning, followed by procession of your personal car and ten Long cars to Grace Crematorium. You will invite those who attend back to your house for buffet, held in your gardens, of course. Balford's will make all arrangements."

"They're the best," he said, smiling at her. "I knew I could depend on you."

"Thank you," she answered, but didn't turn to leave.

"Is there something else?"

"Perhaps this isn't the time to discuss it," she said.

"Now is as good a time as any."

"It's a matter involving the Northern Sector, sir. Apparently some in the Sector are experimenting with natural responses. Sales are down somewhat."

Darren sat back in his chair, leveled his piercing blue eyes on her delicate face, "How far down?"

She turned her eyes from his and murmured, "Not much, sir. Perhaps by a third."

He jumped to his feet bellowing, "You call that not much? Get John Carstair on the phone. He's not doing his job, and this isn't the first time. I want to see him tomorrow morning."

"The funeral is tomorrow morning," she said in a timid voice.

He slammed a fist on his desk. He hated it when anything interfered with business. "When will all this funeral business be over?" he demanded.

"Well, there's the buffet and probably more than a hundred guests," Ms. Claridge said.

He leaned forward and interrupted her, "When?"

She took a step backward. Even after all these years of working for him, she sometimes acted as if she feared his anger. He thought that was a good thing. "When?" he demanded again.

"Probably three-thirty," she said.

"Good. Tell Carstair to be at my house by four. I'll deal with him then."

"Yes, sir," she said and hurried out of the office.

When he was alone, he walked to the wall of windows on his left. It always gave him pleasure to look over the bustling city below. People were working, prospering, loving, and procreating, and they owed it all to him.

Wars and plagues had almost destroyed the world, leaving a desolate and stagnant pool of beings too depressed to care about anything. Governments had failed miserably. He was the one who found the answer in his meager laboratory. Now he ruled a huge empire, governed by figureheads who took their orders from him.

The initial formula had been the tough one. It did away with depression and gave one a feeling of ambition. After that, with minor variations, he could produce a pill for any emotion needed. And all were neatly packaged under the Eberle Emotion Enhancer label. The gratitude of a numbed and dried-out civilization made him the wealthiest man in the world of the twenty-third century.

In the evening Darren took his one pill, cried a sufficient number of tears, and graciously accepted the condolences of friends and neighbors. In the morning he took another pill on his way to the final service at the crematorium. By the time that was over, the effect of the pill had worn off, and he was able to concentrate on the Carstair problem.

The man had to go. Obviously the fool had allowed himself to become addicted to the Well-Being Pill. In that haze he didn't even realize his Sector was losing out. People experimenting with natural emotions were always a threat, but a sharp sales manager could stamp out any such movement with clever ads, special sales, and, of course, the elimination of known leaders in the Natural Response Rebellion.

Carstair's main problem was that he had no stomach for eliminating the enemy. Darren had carefully explained there was no need to get personally involved. There were those on the payroll who took care of such things. Since he refused to order the elimination of rebel leaders, Darren saw only one solution. It was time for Carstair himself to be removed.

On the way back from the crematorium, Darren told his driver to speed ahead of the rest of the procession. He had a phone call to make before his guests arrived. One phone call was all it would take, and Carstair would be out of the way. It was not the first time the elimination of a Sector Manager had become necessary. Darren felt no qualms about giving the order. It was all part of running a business. Suddenly there was a sickening thud, the car swerved, and the driver cursed.

"A dog ran in front of us, sir," the driver said, pulling over.

The driver was checking the front of the car when Darren heard the whining. The dog was still alive. He tried not to listen, but the high, pathetic sound pulled at him.

He had a dog when he was a kid. Rusty. Nothing but a mutt, but smart. Used to follow him everywhere.

Darren got out of the car, walked back to the small furry heap lying by the side of the road. It looked very much like his Rusty. There was a pool of blood forming around its head as the eyes glazed over, and the whining got weaker. The animal sighed deeply, then sank into silence.

Darren could see himself as a ten-year-old, standing in the road, looking down at the limp form of Rusty. The animal's eyes were clouded, but it still looked at him with devotion. Rusty had been hit by a car because his young owner neglected to put him on a leash, but the dog forgave him. Darren shivered as he remembered the loyalty and love Rusty had freely given to him, and the absolute desolation he'd felt as the small creature sighed out its life. He never wanted to feel such agony again.

"Sir, are you all right?"

"Of course I'm all right," Darren shouted and hurried back to the car. "Come on, come on. Let's get going. We can't waste time like this."

"I thought maybe you wanted to take the animal to a veterinarian," the driver said, sneaking a look at him.

"Drive, you fool!" Darren raged. "The dog is dead. The darn dog is dead, and some little brat will be crying his eyes out over him."

"Yes, sir," the driver said, avoiding his employer's eyes in the rearview mirror.

Darren sank back into the soft leather of his seat. He felt suffocated. Perhaps he had been wrong. Maybe the dog still lived, could be saved. Foolish thoughts! Of course the animal was gone, just as Rusty and the young Darren were gone forever. Sentimentality was dangerous.

He took a Well-Being Pill from his pocket and gulped it down. That would calm him, erase all unwanted memories. Its effect would be worn off by the time he had to deal with Carstair at four.

He turned back just once. A small boy was running toward the still body of the dog. For a moment Darren envied the child. He wouldn't need a pill to grieve, but that wouldn't last. Loving parents would not want to see their son suffer. One Well-Being Pill would fix it. The customers were getting younger.

When the car reached his estate, Darren was pleased to see the magnificent buffet Balford's had prepared under an emerald green canopy in the south garden. Ms. Claridge appeared at his elbow. "Mr. Eberle, I'm so glad to see you. Mr. Carstair is here. I distinctly told him his appointment wasn't until four, but he insisted on waiting for you. He's in the library."

Darren was annoyed, but due to the pill he'd taken, he couldn't work himself into anger. No matter. Actually, there was no need to be angry. Pity would be a more suitable emotion. Carstair was doomed and probably knew it. Coming here to plead his case would do him no good.

John Carstair was a big man. He filled the soft leather chair in front of Darren's desk.

"Hello there," he called out as Darren entered the room. "I'm afraid I've upset your efficient Ms. Claridge. Three hours early is more than the poor woman can bear."

"You must be hitting more than the Well-Being Pills," Darren said, frowning. The nerve of this idiot—didn't he know he was in big trouble?

"Now what makes you say a nasty thing like that?" Carstair said.

Darren's own pill was wearing off, and he felt the beginnings of a headache. He should have taken a Tension Reliever before seeing Carstair. "You know damn well what I mean," he shouted at the large man who was smiling at him. There was arrogance in that smile. Darren had the sudden thought that having Carstair at the house early might be the best thing that could have happened.

He went to the chair behind his desk, sat down. "I wanted to see you today, John, because of some disturbing news I've heard about your Sector, but we can talk about it later. In a few moments I'll have quite a few guests here—the funeral, you know."

Carstair nodded his head, "Ah, yes, the funeral. I was sorry to hear about Selena—she was a very nice person. Much nicer than her husband."

Darren chose to ignore the remark. One phone call, and John Carstair was finished. No use arguing with the fool.

"I'll have time for you later, John. We'll talk. Right now I think I should get back to my invited guests."

"I was invited too," Carstair said.

"Not until four o'clock. Just wait here. I'm sure you can find something to read."

With that Darren left the room, slamming the door. He'd wipe that smile off the idiot's face as soon as he could get rid of the other guests. First he made his phone call. "Carstair is here now. Be waiting for him when he leaves. It will be about four fifteen."

When he reached the garden, his guests were arriving. Politely and routinely they expressed their condolences. With equal calm they devoured the spread of food, engaged one another in trivial conversation. It was all very calm and dispassionate, but there were so many of them it was almost four o'clock before the last departed.

Darren hurried back to the library. What if Carstair had skipped out? He needn't have worried. John Carstair's smiling face greeted him when he opened the door.

"All the grieving guests have left the premises, I take it," he said, waving a drink at Darren. "I've taken the liberty of preparing a nice cool drink for both of us."

"I don't need a drink," Darren said.

ALAN YOUNT

Angle of Light in Late Fall

it angles in
   like casting a fishing line out
      an hour before sunset

with a stillness
   from no other season
      light slowing into sandgrain colors

leaves turning above
   and always below
      fish hold steadier

how this
   altered light
      imprints on things

sunlight cast in a mold forever
   like the clear density
      of water

everything you've ever done
   stands out in a fullness
      yet the light also gives off a loss

as the murky emptiness
   and withheld tension
      weighs down the fishing line

in this unending hour
   cottonwoods
      are always rustling

whispering to each other
   memory is the fish not biting
      but always suspended down there

This poem is ALAN YOUNT's ninety-fifth to be published. His poems have appeared most recently in *Big Scream* and *Spring: The Journal of the e.e. cummings Society*.

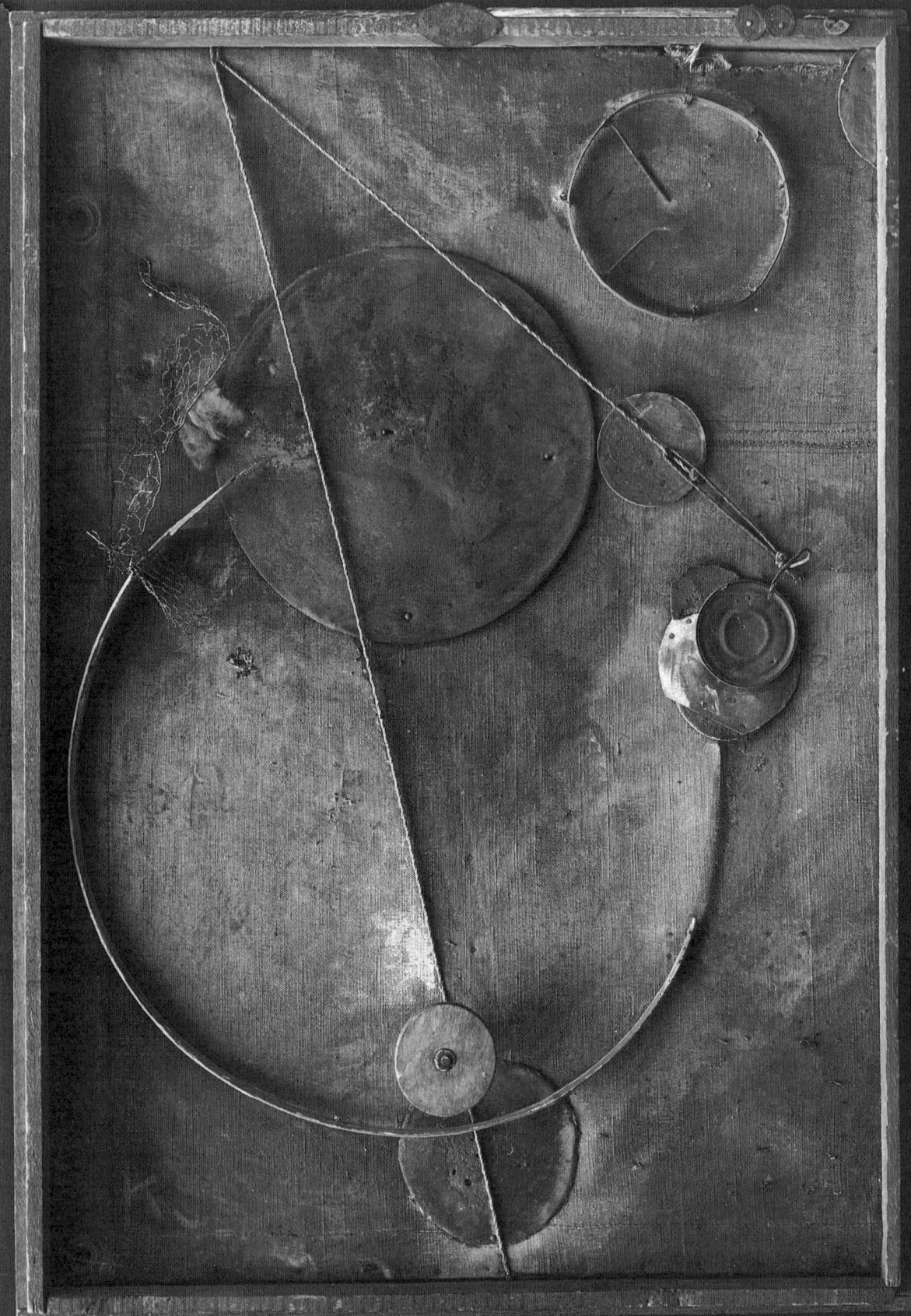

L. ROBERT KECK

Introducing a New Science of Soul

IT IS TIME FOR A BREATH OF FRESH AIR in the realm of the sacred. Stale air not only is unhealthy for inhalation and the continuation of life, it is simply inadequate for the spiritual inspiration that is so desperately needed at this time in history.

It is time for a mind-boggling and spirit-stretching growth-spurt for religions and spiritualities. Arrogance, stagnation, and death are the only alternatives when minds are not humbled by periodic boggling and spirits are not kept fit and flexible with constant stretching.

Oliver Wendell Holmes observed that when a mind is stretched to a new idea, it can never return to its original dimensions. In contrast, however, original dimensions have often been sacrosanct in the realm of the sacred, where religious history, traditional ritual, and ancient spiritual truths have often been the bedrock of inflexibility.

It is time for some new and expansive ideas about God and the Divine-human relationship, ideas that will stretch us beyond where we have been and will not allow us to return to our previous dimensions. That is what growth is all about.

Why We Need a New Science of Soul

WE NEED A NEW SCIENCE OF SOUL precisely because our other sciences have been too materialistic to help us fully understand the territory of Soul. Without denigrating the awesome discoveries that the

Opposite:
Kurt Schwitters.
Revolving [Das Kreisen].
Relief construction of wood, metal, cord, cardboard, wool, wire, leather, and oil on canvas, $43^3/8 \times 35$ in., 1919. The Museum of Modern Art, New York. Advisory Committee Fund. Photograph ©2000 The Museum of Modern Art, New York.

materialistic sciences have made to our understanding of the universe in general and humanity in particular, the fact is that physical evidence alone cannot tell us all there is to know about the human Soul.

For example, materialistic sciences have discovered a great deal about the history of matter but virtually nothing about the history of spirit. They have taught us about the evolution of the human body but not about the evolution of the human Soul. They have examined "Lucy's" skeleton and told us that she was an upstanding relative of ours who lived some three million years ago, but they have not been able to tell us what Lucy valued in her heart. They can tell us that a particular campfire is carbon-dated at 100,000 years ago, but they cannot tell us what the people talked about as they warmed themselves around that campfire on a cool autumn evening. They have discovered our genetic DNA and impressed us with all the potential benefits that can be derived from mapping the human genome, but they have not been able to tell us if there is a spiritual equivalent to DNA, a deep encoding that determines what we value, and why we think and behave in the particular ways that we do. Materialistic science cannot tell us why we conceive of God and create religions in the particular ways that we do, or why those conceptualizations go through changes from time to time.

We need a new kind of science if we are to discover the Soul's DNA, if we are to discover the spiritual equivalent of when humanity began walking upright, discovered spiritual fire, or developed spiritual tools. We need a new kind of science if we are to explore the sacred meaning and purpose within the human journey, to understand what appears to be the current transformation of humanity's Soul, and to speculate reasonably about where religion and spirituality are headed in the future.

Introducing a New Science of Soul: Deep-value Research

"DEEP-VALUES" are the values that are most causal and influential in shaping mainstream human cultures, determining why we think and act in certain ways, and why we create our institutions in the way that we do.

The scope of deep-value research is multinational, interdisciplinary, cross cultural, interracial, and transreligious, because the goal is to discover the common causal influences throughout the human family, and across all the artificial boundaries we have drawn to categorize our living, our thinking, and our research. However, because each culture, each religion, each intellectual discipline has its own language and parochial jargon, a common language was needed—thus, value terminology that crosses all categories.

Deep-value research is not investigating only religion or spirituality. The level of Soul is far more inclusive than that. Contrary to what is generally assumed, deep-values are the cause of religion and spirituality, not the other way around.

Because of their profound influence it is appropriate to refer to deep-values as the DNA of the human Soul. Genetic DNA determines how we look physically, whereas the Soul's DNA determines what we value, how we think, how we act, and why and how we create and run our institutions.

It is also important to be aware of how deep-value research deals with the marvelous diversity that exists throughout the human family. The focus of this research is on identifying and understanding the values that *dominate* the human landscape without denying, ignoring, nor denigrating the exceptions lived out by various individuals, native and indigenous peoples, sub-cultures, and counter-cultures. The hope is that if we can understand why certain values become dominant we might understand why dominant cultures deal with non-dominant cultures in the particular way that they do, and the reasons why majorities treat minorities in the particular way that they do.

You no doubt have noticed that I am capitalizing the word Soul. I do so when referring to the collective human psyche, the deepest part of the human being wherein divine purpose for the species is embedded. When I lowercase the word soul, I am referring to the individual and where her or his spiritual meaning and purpose is accessed. Obviously, to speak of divine purpose in Soul, and in souls, is to make a statement of faith—these are not matters that can be "proven" by the empirical research itself but are, I believe, implied.

Spirituality is our response to the Soul's DNA and our sense of a deep divine meaning and purpose in life. It is here that we begin to see a great deal of differentiation throughout the human family—the same deep-values, the same evolutionary purpose, but a great deal of religious, cultural, and spiritual diversity regarding how individuals and groups choose to respond to that divine presence.

Religion is the more superficial—not to suggest insignificant—and the institutional ways in which groups of people manifest and facilitate their sense of the spiritual, create meaningful community, and honor their particular history, tradition, rituals, and symbol systems.

With these basic concepts in mind, we can proceed in introducing the primary contributions of deep-value research and then briefly summarizing the big picture it presents. We will consider, first of all, how deep-value research enlarges the context, secondly, how it introduces an evolutionary paradigm into the realm of the sacred, and thirdly, how it has discovered periodic punctuations or transformations of the human Soul.

Enlarging the Context

IN RECENT YEARS there has been considerable change in people's tendency to view their own religion as "the one and only true religion," in spite of the current supernova—a bloating but dying star—of fundamentalism. Ecumenical and interfaith dialogue, a shrinking world, along with the greater awareness of humanity's rich diversity of religious and spiritual traditions have all worked to soften the arrogant, exclusivistic, and isolationist propensities of the past.

Deep-value research enlarges the context of the sacred in several ways. It not only respects and honors diversity, it attempts to show precisely why we have experienced such arrogance, exclusivity, and isolation in the former value system, and why they are inconsistent with the emerging value system. But deep-value research makes a particular contribution in expanding the historical context. It probes the question—If we step outside the narrow parameters of any single religion, how far back in history can we find evidence of human spirituality? The quest of that question, via the methodology of deep-value research, has determined that the human Soul awakened about 35,000 ago, which is a considerably larger historical context than what most religions have considered important or relevant.

Introducing an Evolutionary Paradigm

IN ANALYZING THE 35,000-YEAR HISTORY of the human Soul we find fundamental changes. In other words, we find an evolutionary paradigm, in stark contrast to the traditional steady-state paradigm that most religions and spiritualities have embraced. Just as a snapshot in time gives us no clue as to the vast cosmological changes taking place throughout the universe, a truncated historical view of only five thousand years can give religions the illusion that some things are permanent and unchanging when, in fact, they are part of a very long evolutionary process. Soul-time, as cosmological and geological time does, requires a longer history in order to see the changes.

Religions and spiritualities have often exacerbated the problems inherent in a short view of history with an emotional and theological *need* for stasis, stability, dependability, and predictability—in other words, a steady-state paradigm. The science of cosmology, however, provides a marvelous analogy regarding the move from a steady-state into an evolutionary paradigm. It is a particularly ap-

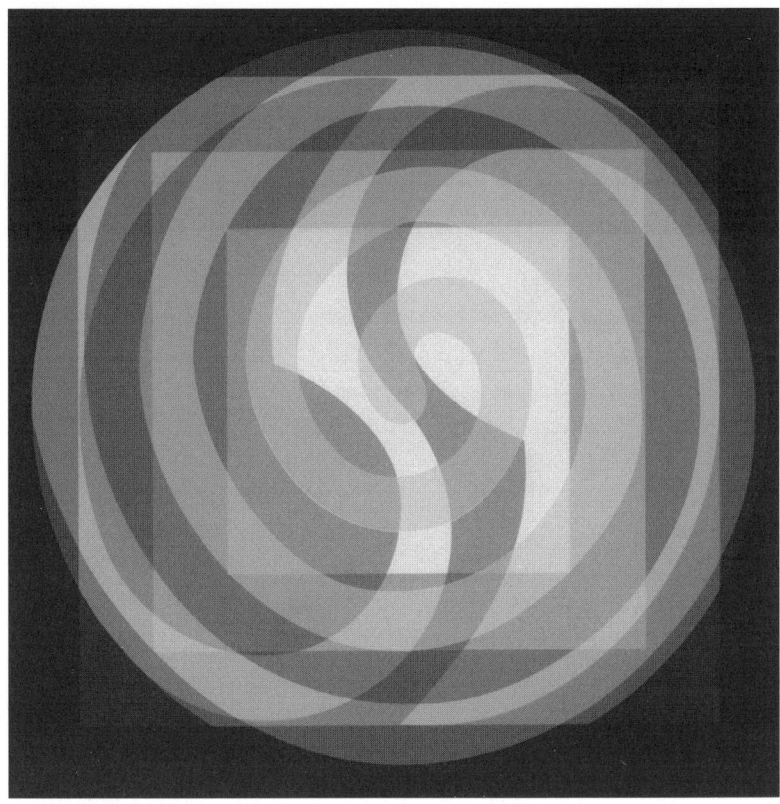

Georges Dremeaux. *Turn, Turn, Turn*. Computer-generated art, 1999.

propriate analogy because cosmology and theology are, in one sense, twins—the former being the way science thinks about the ultimate context in which we live, the latter being the way religion thinks about the ultimate context. In similar fashion, many of us have inserted a theological constant into our spiritual and religious thinking because of our need for God to be stable, static, unchanging, eternal, reliable, and absolutely dependable and predictable.

Early in this century most scientists believed that the universe was in a steady-state—namely, that it was fundamentally stable, dependable, unchanging, and predictable. Albert Einstein, the very name we use to refer to intellectual genius, was one such scientist. So much did Einstein need the universe to be in a steady-state that he actually fudged his mathematics in order to make it so, modifying his General Theory of Relativity by inserting a "cosmological constant." Only after being challenged by other physicists did he admit that his desire for a stable and predictable universe led him into what he personally referred to as "the biggest scientific blunder" of his career.

Deep-value research suggests that we have arrived at the time in humanity's evolutionary journey when the spiritual and religious realms will need to face the same tough growth-spurt that science did a few decades ago, for the history of the human Soul is not a static picture. To the contrary, what we see is a Soul that has been evolving, growing, changing, and in fact, periodically undergoing dramatic transformations.

Periodic Transformations of the Human Soul

DEEP-VALUE RESEARCH has discovered what appears to be a large pattern within the history of the human Soul, a pattern not unlike that discovered within the physical evolutionary sciences.

Paleontologist Stephen Jay Gould, along with his colleague Niles Eldredge, published a paper in 1972 in which they argued that, in contrast to conventional Darwinian gradualism, evolution of the species took place via "punctuated equilibria" (N. Eldredge and S. J. Gould in *Models in Paleobiology*, edited by T. J. M. Schopf, San Francisco: Freeman, Coper and Co., 1972, 82–115). The suggestion was that biological evolution is episodic rather than gradual, jerky rather than smooth, and looking more like stair steps than a ramp. After a period of relative equilibrium—a time in which there was very little change in speciation—evolution was punctuated with a period of dramatic and rapid change. Another period of equilibrium followed, and then another punctuation—the pattern repeating itself over and over again.

In similar fashion, deep-value research suggests that the human Soul goes through periods of relative stasis or equilibrium, only to be punctuated or transformed, and then followed with another period of relative stability. Specifically, after awakening some 35,000 years ago, the human Soul experienced a 25,000 year period of equilibrium, with what appears to be a single evolutionary purpose and a stable deep value system for that entire time. About 10,000 years ago, however, the human Soul was punctuated with its first major transformational change. An entirely new evolutionary purpose displaced the old, and a completely new deep value system emerged to change human cultures. Humanity experienced another period of Soul equilibrium, this time for 10,000 years, bringing us up to our present time. The current chaos that human cultures are experiencing is due to the fact that we are living within another punctuation, the second transformation of Soul.

The implication of this research is that religions and spiritualities will either change in order to resonate with the new and emerging Soul, or they will die. The new Soul will call for a new level of courage—a courageous faith that no longer needs certainty and dogmatic answers, but can embrace uncertainty, novelty, chaos, a sacred seeking and questing after the big questions. And, it is precisely the Soul that we see currently emerging throughout the human family.

The Human Soul: Its Past and Future

THE EVIDENCE GLEANED FROM DEEP-VALUE RESEARCH seems to be communicated best with a maturational metaphor. As with an individual, humanity experienced a childhood epoch with a particular developmental purpose, followed by an adolescent epoch with its own unique maturational agenda, and now appears to be entering its adult epoch with a new and different purpose. Each evolutionary epoch with its special developmental purpose also has a unique deep-value system with which to facilitate that purpose. In summary, then, the big picture of human spiritual evolution looks as follows:

The human Soul apparently awakened about 35,000 years ago with a deep-value system that capped off a very long childhood epoch of physiological evolution. Value systems included, first of all, a celebration of human at-one-ment with nature in general and a profound respect for animal powers in particular. Our childhood, if you will, was spent in the arms of Mother Earth and with a close communion with our brothers and sisters of other species.

The second deep value of Epoch I, a natural extension from the first, celebrated and focused on the feminine side of Soul. We did not know of paternity at that time, and the woman was the most obvious giver and nurturer of life. It is not surprising, therefore, that when our religious impulse emerged, when we began to think about giving praise and worship to the divine energy that empowered all of life, we conceived of divinity as an Earth Goddess.

The third deep value was that of non-violence. As incredible as that may sound to our 21st century ears, we now have a rather considerable body of evidence that suggests that it was a much more non-violent epoch than what we have known and experienced in recent millennia. For instance, in the art of this twenty-five thousand year period, we find no depictions of war, no celebration of warrior-priests, and no evidence of human or animal sacrifice. Contrast that with the art of recent millennia. One does not have to overly romanticize humanity's first epoch of Soul to realize that the ethic of relationship was quite different.

Ten thousand years ago the human Soul experienced its first transformation. It was time in our evolutionary journey for our species to move from childhood into adolescence. The developmental agenda, in turn, shifted from physiological to psychological. We had grown a human body and it was now time to grow a human ego and mind. Consequently, a completely new deep-value system replaced the old so that the new evolutionary purpose could be carried to the surface of culture and change humanity's ways of thinking and acting.

With ego development coming center-stage, the first deep-value to emerge from humanity's new Soul was that of a changed relationship with nature. Just as an individual develops his or her ego by distinguishing "self" from "other," humanity distinguished itself from the rest of nature. The human-nature unity was broken. The relationship was changed from one of cooperation to one of separation, manipulation, management, control, use and abuse. This was when agriculture, horticulture, and animal husbandry began. And, this perception of distinction was what eventually led to a human lifestyle that treated nature as an adolescent treats the 'fridge'—a handy resource for whatever we were hungry for, and we expected "Mom" to keep it stocked! Only when this ten thousand year old value began to die in the latter half of the twentieth century did humanity, generally speaking, become aware of how such an immature relationship was simply unsustainable.

Reducing the whole of human-nature into the presumed separate and distinct parts of humanity and nature launched an epoch-long habit of reductionism—reducing wholes to parts and then giving emphasis to the part while forgetting about the whole. We've seen it shape our health-care, our educational systems, our research projects, and our religions. It created a prism through which we viewed the world—a prism of isms—leading to sexism, racism, nationalism, etc.

As pervasive as reductionism has been in shaping modern human cultures, the most crucial consequence of separating humanity from nature was in our Soul. By becoming estranged from nature, humanity became estranged from the feminine side of Soul. In other words, we reduced the whole of Soul into gender pieces, elevated the masculine and sublimated the feminine. It made the subsequent deep values of patriarchy and hierarchy inevitable. In addition, by becoming estranged from our natural power base, nature itself, we became habituated into an immature and distorted expression of power—either projecting all essential power externally, and/or considering the evidence of power to be that of controlling other people, money, land, and the possession of privileged knowledge. The deep-values of power and control served imperialistic institutions that demanded subservience and conformity to rigid belief systems and ways of living. Eventually, horrendous amounts of violence were used to enforce and manifest such power and control. It was the self-proclaimed right to Manifest Destiny.

Today we are living within only the second punctuation of Soul in humanity's entire evolutionary journey. No wonder we experience such chaos, such birthing and dying, within the womb/tomb of a Soul in transformation. It can be a very confusing time when trying to differentiate what is dying from what is being born, when discerning the deconstruction from the reconstruction, and the devolution from the evolution.

Deep-value research, however, provides insight into the meaning and purpose of this chaotic time. Just as the new science of Chaos points to an underlying unity, deep-value research reveals a profoundly unifying pattern within the chaos of a Soul in transformation. In addition, deep-value research gives us a glimpse into the future by exploring how the new emergent value system will change the way we think, act, and create and run our institutions.

Undoubtedly the most important deep-value that is currently emerging from humanity's Soul to shape and characterize Epoch III is that of re-membering what we dismembered ten thousand years ago, humanity and nature. It will, in the process, redefine human nature. We should not underestimate the extent to which this will change us. Environmentalism and ecological awareness are but early ripples of this wave of the future. Patriarchal institutions are "history," for example, precisely because their time in history is over. In Epoch III a whole-Souled humanity simply will not tolerate the diminishment of human potential that results when one gender is elevated over another—or, for that matter, whenever any group is elevated over another.

The ubiquity of wholeness is the second emergent deep-value. The sciences of the last century, overturning some of the pet theories of classical science, have been the primary discoverers and proponents of how everything in the universe is interconnected and interrelated. The theological implications of this deep-value will dramatically change the ways in which we have traditionally thought about the divine-human relationship, and a maturation and priority of love and compassion is the spiritual energy of wholeness. In one respect, that doesn't sound like new information. We have given lip-service to love for a long time, but as Paul Tillich once put it, we will eventually discover that it is not an emotional power but an ontological one—"the dynamic reunion of that which has been separated." We simply could not fully understand the power of love when we were in our adolescent epoch, but spiritual maturation will enable that discovery.

The third new deep-value of Epoch III is the democratization of power. We will discover how essential power is not handed down from on high or conferred on us from external authorities—it is an emergent quality from within the individual, and from within the relationships between and coalitions of individuals.

The fourth and final Epoch III deep-value—what will probably be the most controversial—is the spirituality of time. Religious and/or spiritual people may have a particularly difficult time with this one, precisely because of our long-held assumptions that time was relevant only in human realms, whereas God, Heaven, Nirvana, etc. are presumably outside of time, above it all, eternal, and unchanging. We have had a need for theological constants. Nevertheless, the expansive vision of the divine-human relationship will have a new respect for the spirituality that is within the flow of time—thus, novelty, creativity, growth, development, chaos, disorder, change, maturation, and process will become central players in the sacred evolution of life.

"There is a grandeur in this view of life."

With those words Charles Darwin began the final sentence of his book, *The Origin of Species.* However, If there is a grandeur in biological evolution, how much more grand it is to consider a synthesis of physical, mental, and spiritual evolution. If there is a grandeur in physical development, how much more so in spiritual maturation. For it is the Soul that gives birth to and embraces our very sense of grandeur. It is the Soul that provides humanity with an oceanic, even a cosmic, view of life.

Deep-value research has discovered a grand evolutionary history of the human Soul, a grand maturational process of human growth and development, and a future that promises potential grandeur beyond our imaginations. We can choose to resist those evolutionary energies, or we can resonate and cooperate with them. And that, my friends, is the choice of a lifetime.

L. ROBERT KECK holds a master's degree in theology from Vanderbilt University and a doctorate in the philosophy of health from Union Graduate School. Professionally he has served as a United Methodist minister on the faculty of the Ohio State University medical school, and as president of Boulder Graduate School. Currently he is an independent scholar, a philosopher of health, an evolutionary theologian, and the creator of deep-value research. This essay is adapted from his book, *Sacred Quest: The Evolution and Future of the Human Soul,* recently published by the Swedenborg Foundation's imprint, Chrysalis Books.